# growing
## a definition of poetry


isbn: 978-1-3999-9519-1

to my sister Chantelle, for growing with me throughout this book. your strength could move mountains, it most certainly has moved mine.

## trigger warnings:

throughout the book there are mentions of mental health, eating disorders, body dysmorphia and sexual assault.

please be kind to yourself and reach out to someone if you are struggling.

this book will be waiting for you when you are ready.

growing takes a lot of reflection.

perhaps now it is time to look into the mirrors of your life…

this chapter illustrates the ease of succumbing to immaturity as you begin your twenties.

I told myself *you're still young, you can fuck up once in a while* but I wish I learnt how to balance caution with courage.

these next few pages are not entirely poetic; they are laced with anger, envy and self-sabotage (traits that we frown upon despite them being ubiquitous).

I ended up seeking safety in everything detrimental because I believed myself to be an exception to their consequences.

what I wish I knew then was that the intrinsic part of human nature is imperfection. mistakes are inevitable and not entirely negative in their existence; after all, they help shape us into who we are meant to be.

but that is all part of *growing up*, right?

# Growing Up

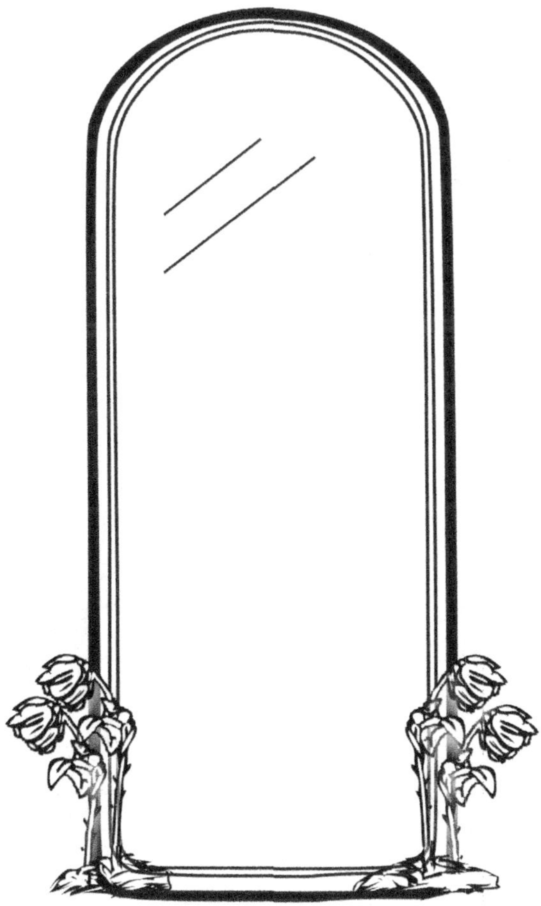

I bought myself flowers

their crimson smiles beaming
as their lips kissed the earth
and continued to grow

but then life got in the way
and I couldn't remember
to pour sun into the vase

so their petals became withered
their little bodies shivering
as their wide eyes stared up at me

*I'm sorry I couldn't save you* I whisper
*I could barely save myself*

sometimes I don't want to be here

more so in the sense of being *physical*

I embody all of love's losses
and I have become divisible
to the thoughts that lose me

they clutch at my limbs
and extend them in a reach
to be something more

and I cannot keep yearning

it is tearing me into mosaics
and I can't keep letting my pain
bleed into my art like it is normal

I don't want to feel anymore

there are moments where I feel as though I will never belong. a brief glimpse of existence washes over me with purpose and then the tide breaks, and the earth falls and I am left floating in space watching planets become full, too full for me to be wanted.

- *that's the only thing you are good for*

what if I have lost myself
in the endless need to be distracted
the way I've acted
is a reflection of who I never wanted to be

you see
I never understood the phrase
*hurt people hurt people*
but now it relates back to me

practically I cannot sustain
causing pain because it avoids my own
I am not at home
in acting this way
but I'm afraid you won't stay
if I show you who I really am

people say they will
people say they can
but the six year plan I trusted
rusted and crumbled beneath me

so forgive me if I don't trust people completely

I saw you, boasting loudly with humour, and it was like seeing another version of myself. you covered yourself in laughs to distract from insecurity, playing it off like you were always naturally *that funny.* from that point onwards I knew that I was meant to know you.

*it seemed like we were tied together*

we started off innocent, two children unaware they were going to grow into two adults. we lived separate existences but laughed and argued together; we spat and we spited, we cried and we ignited the sparks that we both tried to hide.

*and then I hurt you*

I let you break your walls down, I clawed the fragile pieces of your heart into shards and then decided to find a man who was better than you. we did not speak from then onwards; we threw fists with knuckles that bled from emotion.

*we did this for years*

then maturity rolled over us like a gentle wave and we realised we could laugh together again. we then laughed a little too loudly and found our hearts racing faster.

*and so you left*

I understood why; I had someone in my life that I could lose you from thought and pretend like nothing happened. you had yourself which is enough entirely on its own but could not fill the hole that love left you. time glided through and you forgave me for unconsciously loving you and we let the platonic nature of our love tear apart the romantic aspect that had been sitting there for years.

*until he left me*

after six years this seemed to be our time; we were adults now. though mature, we still swapped love for lust. we covered ourselves in seduction and I avoided the introduction of what we could be. you brought it to the surface and I lost myself at sea; I did not want to hurt again so I drowned our potential.

and I hurt you
*again*

and so you left
*again*

and we became untied
only this time
*for good*

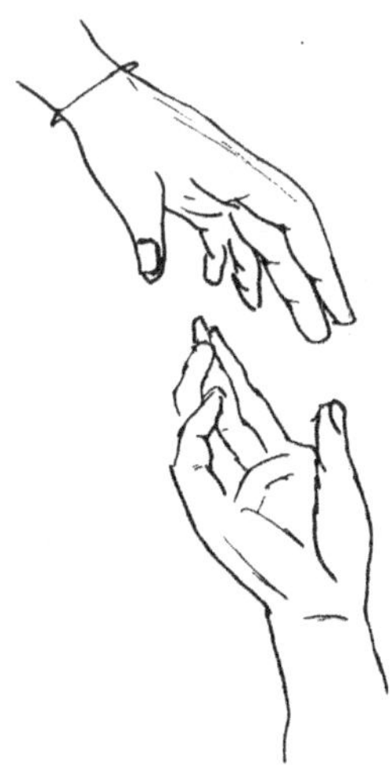

Machiavelli decided
there were two roads
love or fear

I chose the latter

so when you walked through
I manipulated you
to suit my needs
letting you fear
the truth from me

*we all have dark interiors*

and it worked
for a while

until I stopped looking
and the ground beneath me
became a soft green
and I was running towards love
blindly and unseen
and I loved you like
nothing from before
but I had to leave
because I couldn't breathe
to give you any more

I promised myself
the season of sun and sabotage
had been swallowed by September

but parts of the pain clung to the way
I let you fall for me only to leave you
burning in my ember

you met me at the station
hopefully holding those roses
that I know I'll always remember

but I could see the stems sink
and I couldn't help but think
I should have left you in December

one shot then another
let me drink my woes away
blackout another night
I'll forget the next day

*a party next weekend?*
I will be the last to leave
pour me another glass
this is the way I breathe

pictures the next morning
about how I was last night
I do not pretend to be moral
I am not trying to act right

more shots, let's buy a bottle
crack it open to forget
let me soak up my sorrow
let us drink to regret

drunken waves fog my mind
take a shot and fight a line
lose myself by the morning
there is a self that I am mourning

I stand at her grave and weep
broke the promises she'd keep
burn the path, watch the flame
I hate the fact I welcomed change

because now it is simple to be hated
I slip away intoxicated
I melt myself into cold bodies
then it hits and I am sorry

there is nowhere I can run
I hate the girl I have become
she is scared to her core
and so she recklessly hurts to be cared for

I lost sight of who I was
in the urgency to be someone else

I do not recognise
my reflection anymore
sure, there is a detection
of a girl from before
but she is altered
and changed by time

I cannot find her
in what she's left behind

I fall into the arms of addiction
as though it is an old friend

I pretend as if it wants the best for me
as if this is a test for me
swapping pain for addiction
swapping reality for a fiction
I have created in the safety
of my harmful home

for here I am not alone in my pain
but transported to a fantasy
that sets me free from reality
and allows me to breathe
allows me to leave the world of hatred
into one I have created
in the security of false promises

if I am honest
I know what I have built
is a result of lost guilt
that I have tried to erase
but instead misplaced
in the cracks of my brain

and I cannot explain
why I allow myself to become a contradiction
but I'd rather trade this pain
for a taste of that sweet addiction

*I don't take shit from anyone anymore*

I treat them with the respect
they forget they gave me before
and then they start bluffing
hate that I meet them
with the same nothing
they gave me
they blame me
when the truth is as clear as day

that I needed you and you just walked away

as if my heart didn't go missing
as if I wasn't wishing in between my sobs
as if I didn't beg for this pain to stop

as if I didn't ask for you to be there

so now I act with the same care
you gave me
do not blame me
for being heartless
when I was once heartfelt

if the finger is to be pointed
make sure it is at yourself

I silence impulsivity
with growth and experience
trying to inhibit everything I know
with everything I should be

there are expectations
expecting me
but I don’t know how to reach them
when everyone is growing

and I’m only showing a sign of decline
acting on ideas that aren’t even mine
but seem to work well within a time
of the present but it doesn’t last
and I’m left wishing for the past
that doesn’t come

I’m someone I don’t even like
and I’m slightly confused
with how easily I accept being used
to ensure I’m not alone

I silence impulsivity
with these men on my phone
who mean nothing
I am bluffing

*I am only something*
*when someone tells me I’m enough*

I don’t feel ready for love
but I am searching
unearthing the world
to silence the girl
who is hurting

she is deserving of more
than I give her
I don't forgive her
for what she is doing

she is pursuing a life
of short term distractions
reckless attractions
that fade into pain

why trust again
when lusting feels the same
but hurts a whole lot less

I am doing my best
to be better
but everything I do upsets her
and I don't know how to get back to before
and ensure I work things through

I am scared deep down
I'm doing this to go back to you

I sought the crave of comfort so wildly
that I came upon ravenous men
who spoke rough words of lust
to make me fond of them

for a while it was sufficient
until I identified it a bore
with bright lights and late nights
I thought of you and sought some more

emotions were pulled from the dark
though not long did they remain
I fumbled with my confused thoughts
until I stumbled upon you again

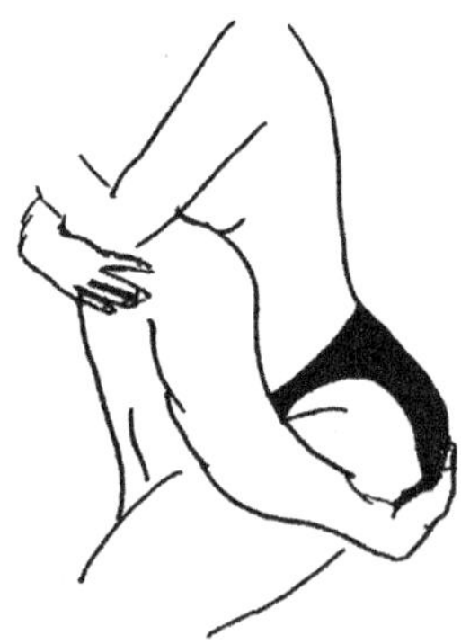

adulthood is a scam

when you're younger you crave it
when you're older you try to escape it

I should have read the terms and conditions
I should have listened
when they said to stay a child
to not grow up

not run to towards maturity and love
because when you're in it, you're stuck
and no one gives a fuck

because this is the
next part of life, right?
and you're expected
to do it right, right?

but what if you do it wrong?

what if you don't know
the next lyric to the song?

what if you only just realised
adulthood was a scam
and you didn't have a plan
because you thought you had time

but now all you hear is
a clock, ticking, ticking
and the key collides with
a lock, clicking, clicking
and all your mistakes are
now sticking, sticking
and there are choices to be made

start picking, picking

but what if I pick the wrong one?
what if I try and try and
I never end up being someone?
what if all I've done is a
certificate and a dream?
what if I am loose, becoming
unthreaded from a seam?

it seems as though we exist
through a kaleidoscope
a sky of hope
painted by the innocence of age
and when we become old enough
we turn a new page
and the sky scopes
shattering the kaleidoscope

blind until vision
open to ambition
until the close of collision
tells you to make a decision
to just grow up

they did not say that when you're grown,
the world becomes more unknown
than when you knew less

back then you did not need to repress

you lived in harmony with your own dreams
eating ice cream without knowing of health
asking for presents without knowing of wealth

living because you could
not because you should

not wondering what would happen
if it all just stopped
not wondering why I always
hear that clock ticking away

grow up they say
the time to be is now
grow up, they say

my only response is how?

I used to inject male validation
as if it was heroine
it was just as addictive
but far less genuine

for at least the buzz
of a drug is predictable
but the fuss from a man
is irregularly irresistible

when their compliments
are laced with drunken breath
you fall for their words
right when you should have left
but that is not to say
the blame falls solely on your shoulders
you learn to know the truth
of youth when you're older

that women were taught to seek
the approval of men
because then we'd survive
at the dominating hands of them
because what is a woman
without a man to let her live
what was Eve if not the product
of Adam's spare rib?

I feel so alone
tied to a phone
that holds no substance

I wait for texts
but don't reply
I don't know why
my life is tied to this box

but I can't stop
mind numbingly scrolling
enrolling myself into a digital fantasy
to distract from the loneliness of my reality

but notifications
are imitations
of true intimacy

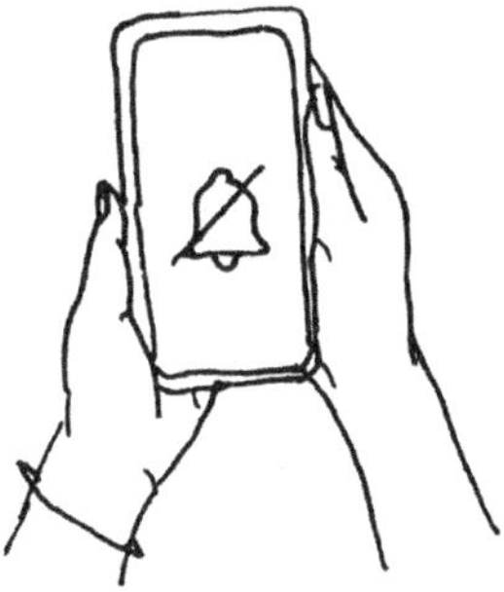

and I still feel lost
after what you did to me

you left me naked
with my fears
abandoned me
after six years
and best believe it hurts

I don't know what I deserve
but it isn't holding onto a feed
to erase the need of you
though I'm finally free of you
I haven't a clue what to do
in terms of navigation
I guess the start of all this healing
is to turn off the notifications

*my mother didn't warn me about you*

she used to laugh with you
when we sat in the back of the car
though it wasn't much effort
because you didn't live very far
but she'd always sing your praises
she'd always ask how you were
so when you left me alone
you also managed to hurt her

our friendship became overgrown

I tried my best
to style it back to spring
but you left it to wither
leaving me with nothing
but broken branches
and loosening leaves
every thorn cut deep but
you plucked them with ease

*you left*

and still I chased you
with a heart that could plead
I wanted to bring this back
somehow replant the seed

but you left me alone
with nothing but
overgrown memories

there is a graveyard on my wall

pictures of faces
who cannot even tell you
where I'm living now

smiles trapped in time
lost from the present
buried in the past

I walk through the tombs
yearning for the life
behind the lens

*I think I'm mourning who we used to be*

this may be my hometown
but it isn't my home anymore

it is a relic of what was
a tomb of the time before

it is a cemetery of memory
where I mourn through
buildings that are much more
than bricks and stone

they house laughter and love
within bars and comedy clubs
they hold promises I thought
were much bigger than us

the cracks in the concrete
covet the hope I left behind
the restaurant and its waiters
remember you were kind

they remain stuck in what we left
in the play that was shown
so perhaps it is my hometown
but this graveyard is not my home

I hold myself close to you

well as close as you can
when watching life play out
through a window

I let my fingertips shiver
at the touch of the glass
nose and lips pressed against it
to make the moment last

*let me in*
*please just let me in*

I never understood first dates in the cinema

dark lights, loud sounds
that weren't your own
perhaps fingers would touch
but that was the joy alone
no conversation, no connection
just two people lost in uncomfortable seats

can you really say you've met
in a place you cannot truly meet?

I still do not know where I am

I am lonely and broken
I say words but feel they're not spoken
and I miss knowing where I am supposed to go

I miss who I was before I had to let go

because now I don't know who I am
I don't know if I can keep on pretending

because it hurts

and I deserve to feel at home
but I roam and I roam and I roam
and there are just four walls and lost hearts
there are people to be loved
but they tear us all apart

and I don't want to be pessimistic

saying the bullshit that negativity is realistic
because I don't believe that
I buy into love and light
my heart is hurting
but I know that after night
will come day

and I won't always feel this way

I don't know where I am
or where I am going
but I know it will all be okay

if my October self walked up to me now
and asked how it all worked out
I would merely say that it did

I wouldn't waste my breath
telling her that you left
I simply would not reply
and when she asks why
I will tell her that there is no point in revealing
the truth to her future healing
because why spoil something so beautiful?

why tell her the truth at all
when she can live in a lie
she doesn't recognise is a fantasy
why destroy her reality
that she is so happy within
why tear her skin into two
when you are planning on doing it too?

I tell myself *I am growing up*
and somehow my hands no longer shake
at the thought of time passing
for there is something comforting
in becoming who I always wanted to

growing - a definition of poetry

this chapter is here to validate the ache of modern day dating.

I entered the realm of *situationships* completely clueless. I did not know that someone could give you everything and nothing simultaneously. I did not know that I would fall for it. I saw the red flags and believed I would be the one who could find out how to turn them green.

the truth is though, you cannot change people into who you want them to be. you cannot love someone into being worthy of you, nor should you want to. someone who loves will not ask you to neglect your heart's needs to make them comfortable. someone who loves you will not be content with giving you the bare minimum. someone who loves you would not make you feel like this.

but that's all part of *growing apart*, right?

# Growing Apart

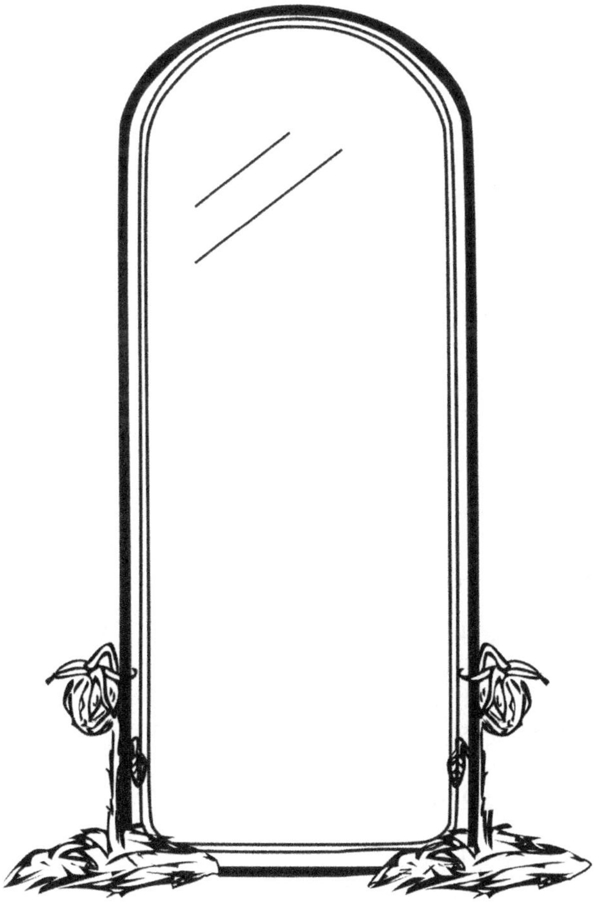

<u>the first time I took you back</u>
they called me hopeful
*a dreamer who could see*
*anything in the clouds*
*except the rain*
but you opened an umbrella

only to leave again

and I stopped dreaming
started sleeping
only to awake to the
nightmare of a reality
without you

I was alone again

<u>the second time I took you back</u>
there were whispers
*she'd break her own heart*
*if it meant she was loved*
but you told me not to listen

until you left again

and this time there was anger
a broken flame turning the
butterflies in my stomach
into swollen ash

I think they got the easy way out

<u>the third time I took you back</u>
they told me I was easy
*a punchbag waiting to be hit*
but there was nothing easy

about loving you
or losing you
or breaking every part of me
to somehow fix the broken parts of you

it wasn't easy

and that's when I realised
I couldn't stay anymore

my first language is poetry

so falling in love with a man
who could not communicate
felt like a pen running out of ink

he bled me dry
whilst I fed him metaphors
and he simply spat them out
into piles of jumbled lines

as if I didn't pour myself
into each stanza that I gave him
or into every rhyme
that he didn't even read

and so I started translating
my verses into prose
he told me to stop the fiction
and I listened, I suppose

I forgot how to inspire
but he told me this was better
and so when he left there was no ink
just an unopened love letter

alcohol makes the wounds deeper
but it sure tastes sweeter
than remembering you

you can wound me
as long as you consume me
skin touching skin
I long for you to use me
as long as you stay
there is nothing to me
don’t leave, my lust
you are not through with me

I'd rather be hated
by you than loved

it's easier, sharper
I can predict the ending
the softer silences
take longer when mending
and so I can sit with this
be okay with the pain
because at least then
I can't lose myself again

when you walk all over me
I let your footprints dent me
because I only ever wanted
to be your foundation

I'm sure he likes me
but it feels like a chore
like I'm nothing more
than "a girl with a lot of love
and a good set of tits"
nothing more, nothing less

*will he ever commit?*

*I miss you*

my phone lights up
and I can't help but sigh

*I miss you too*

fuck, why do I reply?

I was enough back then

wide-eyed, trusting and sure
I gave you everything I had
and whilst I understand your fear
I couldn't see why love was bad

but once you ran from potential
it took a few months to see
that everything you feared
you loved to find in me

but what if now I am you
and I fear falling fast
I don't know if I want this
can I really make us last?

but I smile as your name
lights the darkness on my phone
what if you are the answer
to make my world a little less alone?

you tell me you love me

it's only been weeks
but we speak
and it's like fate
has fallen at my feet

you tell me that meeting me
has put your world onto balance
an equilibrium has happened
and I'm exactly where you want to be

you seem like everything
I told you I wanted for me

you tell me this is not lust
it's love and to trust
and so suddenly
I let you in

and then we end
as soon as we begin

I let my armour fall
I give you my all
until you leave me bare
you wanted me
until I started to care
and once I did
you left me there
in the rubble of love bombing
longing for the person you never were

we were never together
and I suppose that is the issue

this is not a break up
or a break down
because you cannot break
what was never whole to begin with

yet I am glued to my bed
stuck to my thoughts
too scared to tear myself away
from the fear I will not recover
whilst you briskly find yourself
striding in the streets of France

*how ironic that you find yourself*
*in the city of which stands for*
*everything you fear the most*

we tiptoe around the truth
blaming the cages of our youth
because it easier than admitting
that we both fear committing
and so we sit here living
in this state of friends and lovers
probably talking to others
but only under covers together
I can't promise you forever
or say that you'll be mine
but I can promise tonight
you'll have a good time

when you tell me you are leaving
I let my heart bleed into metaphors
and I write this pain into existence
so at least something about us was real

this pen is my anchor
this ink is my lifeline
this keyboard is my home
this poem is all mine

but I said the same about you

so perhaps my poetry
is not even true

there isn't much to say
but I'd rather we stay
and ride this carousel
listening to you yell
at me on repeat
then complete
whatever this is

how it feels to watch them leave…

you allow the sadness to rest its head momentarily; you stroke its hair, hold its hand and whisper it comfort. you hold it for everything it feels. you cannot run from the discomfort of its truth - that this sadness is the last thing you have left of them. you would rather have something than nothing even if it kills you.

the nights ache with the memory of their laughter, their scent that reminds you of faint vanilla and home, their touch that feels like it's been tattooed within your skin. the nights aches to make them a memory. you ache because you can no longer love them how you used to. you would rather have something than nothing even if it kills you.

*and it's killing you, isn't it?*

my mood is dependant
on the way your fingers
embrace the keyboard

I am tangled in your tone

knotted in the time it takes
for you to acknowledge me

will I ever be able to
untangle my worth from you?

I cannot keep writing poetry about you
if I do not occupy your thoughts

I ought to write about him or her
but they blur into a hole of
everything that isn't you

I know your eye wanders

I don't resist your promiscuity
I admit my insecurity
and let myself sit comfortably
in the fact you have already hurt me

I cannot be surprised
if your head turns to the exit sign
because you were never mine to begin with

*it's safer this way*

an apology does not make
what you did okay

it does not pick up the pieces
of my heart and put it back together
it does not build up the trust
of when you said we would be forever

it does not mend the insecurity
that you swore was wrong to feel
when you said you were sorry
was that also as real

as the month you spent debating
whether staying with me was worth it
you used me in that time
called me mine and then deserted

*I don't deserve it*

you don't get to apologise
because sorry is not enough
sorry does not fix
how you made me fall in love
with our past
our present
and most definitely future

I held on to what we said
you let go
and I had no clue
because I swore
it would always be you

my heart is not a game to play with
yet it is your turn to serve
but you swerve in and out of conditions

you do not listen
but I do not speak
I do not want to seem weak
when you have appeared okay

day by day
I wait for the text
the resurrection of the ex
but it never arrives
and I realise
you will not fulfil your promises

why am I surprised
that you are not honest
when you broke my heart
into a million pieces

I know I should have seen it coming
this person you're becoming
but I am shocked that this
is how you'd leave us

I sit here and read my poetry
as though you wrote it

I hope it somehow transcends
and I pretend that you still care
even though you aren't there anymore
even though we will never be
what we were before

I still dream

and it may seem
like I'm still hoping
I'm not, I'm just coping
of going into life without
the person I thought would complete it

you can't just delete it
merely because they leave
life doesn't simply freeze
the moments and put it in the past
if they truly matter then their love
will last beyond their stay

just because you left
doesn't mean you're gone away

and I go to say little things
that only you would get
and for a moment I forget
we aren't together

and that's not to say
that I ever want us back
it's just hard to not say
little things that only you would understand

strip me down to organs
and watch how my blood
will pump for you

step on my lungs
and drink the air
abandoning my throat

take everything
and leave me empty
waiting to be filled by you

I hold onto the good parts of you
until they burn cuts into my skin
I hope a better version into existence
believing it'll change everything

but it never does

I cannot put you back together
when you cannot admit you're broken
I cannot love you into kindness
when you bleed their wounds open

*I cannot change you*

you are every part as hurtful
as you were when you left
but I hope you find some peace
and lay your dark soul to rest

we are hanging on to each other
knowing that it will hurt fiercely
if we rip away from our potential

the loss will leave us empty
as we bleed out vacancy
into this new foundation

*but could something else grow here?*

something whole
something safe
something secure

something more than what we could be

perhaps this love is a loose tooth
needing to be lost
for another to be set free

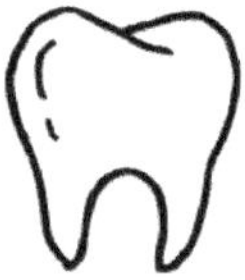

I fall back
into your eyes
because they're the
only hue I recognise

I listen to the
lyrics of our song
because when I first heard it
you did nothing wrong

I wear your
tired old sweater
breathing in the only
scent I can remember

I do anything
and almost everything
to bring us back together

you wear the blame comfortably
after all, it fits you right

but forgiveness is coming up short
it seems to sit too tight

and I try to release the loss
but this forcefield is magnetic

but you left like I was nothing
and I don't think I can forget it

you could have stayed

no one told you to leave
no one grabbed my lungs
and forced you to squeeze

but that is exactly what you did

stealing my final breath
you promised me heaven
but couldn't even give me death
and now there is nothing left but this

loving isn't a choice but leaving is

and I cannot change
what you choose
you promised to stay
but had nothing to prove
except how wrong I was
in trusting you

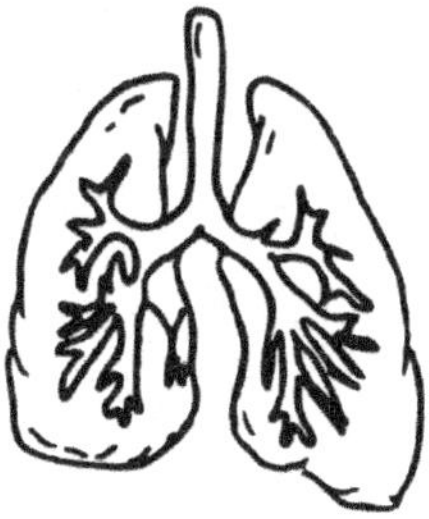

## *she is just a friend*

you said this with such conviction
so how could I not listen
when you held my cheek in your hand
and told me the only plans you had

were for you and I

but I suppose you didn't
finish that sentence
for you never mentioned
how it would be

you and I and her

the rest seems like a lost blur
filled with clouds of insecurity
you ensuring me
that it was all in my head
whilst she was in your bed

you and her and

I was left behind

## to the girl he cheated on me with

you didn't know I existed
for a while I didn't know you existed too
but when I did I went to blame you

and *I am sorry*

I felt the quintessential 'girls against girls'
narrative drilled into my soft skin
and so my loathing forgot him and found you

and I am sorry for everything I said about you

jealousy burned in my veins
and so I found every one of my faults
in the soft glow of your perfection

but I hope you know I don't blame you

I hope the guilt curls inside him
as he recalls the dreams he sold
to us during those late night calls
I hope he regrets it all

because we deserve better than him

I let go of the invisible string
that led our lives to exist together
but somehow I'm still tangled in knots
and I cannot stop

thinking about you

my heart may ache a little less
when someone mentions your name
but our string is still caught up
in all my attempts to change
and I cannot stop

thinking about you

we used to let dreams form
between whispered kisses

you would be a lawyer
I'd be a poet

soft rain intertwined with the sun
and we promised to be there
for when we became someone

we were supposed to do it together

but now we are separated by the
distance of miles and memories
that are aching to tell you I made it

I broke my rules for you

I bent my back
and all the values it held
in hopes to please you

I plucked my heart strings
to the beat of your melody
tuned to your way of living

I lost myself
in hopes you'd find
yourself in me

and you never did

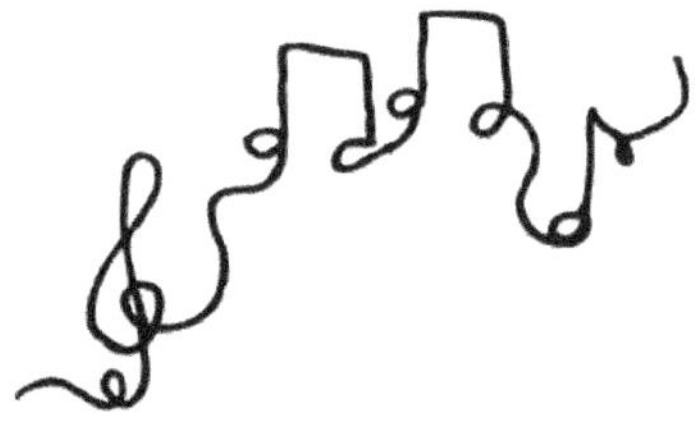

I don't want to wait to love you
to hesitate to trust you
to wonder if lust will fall to love
to wander from me and you into us

I don't want to hold back
to let my words smack
against the back of my throat

I don't want to choke
on my letters
I don't feel better
keeping it all in

I just want to tell you everything

a part of me knows
he knows and doesn't care

a part of me knows
he doesn't bother to show up
even when he's there

a part of me knows
that he'll never meet me
exactly half way

and a part of me knows
he is not the one
who will stay

but I stay
and in every way
I am there
and I care

knowing he will
never do the same

I'll keep the light on
just in case you ever find home
in the safety of these four walls again

all I wanted is for you to care
to think of me without prompt

to just *want* me

and somehow that was
still too big of an ask
still too big of a task
for you to do

the truth is you never loved me
the way that I loved you

*no, it's fine*

it's easier to tell you it's okay
than to confess that you
made me feel insignificant

every silence made my mind bleed
with questions as to why
I would ever be good enough for you

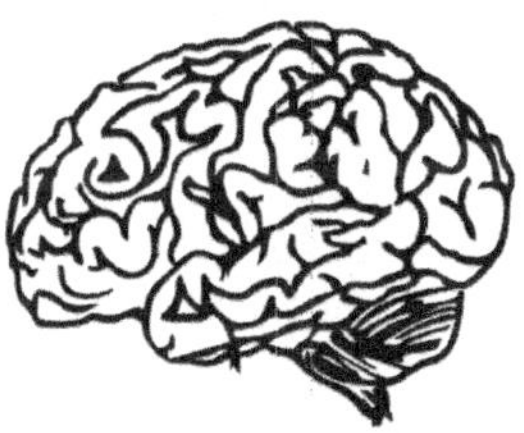

I thought I could fix you

I thought the issue
was the lack of attempt
I thought it meant
that I would be
the one to change you
to rearrange you
into the perfect shape
of who I wanted you to be

I realise now that
that wasn't healthy for you
nor was it healthy for me

you put in the bare minimum

*the bare fucking minimum*

and I fall at your feet
telling the people I meet
of this guy that I met
that I can't seem to forget

I used to think
I would regret
falling for you
but it's not true

I love in the way that I do
and I won't change it for any man
I won't change it for you

but I'll keep my standards
raised high with intention
I'll mention that you need
to pick the bar off the floor
and set it where it should stand

maybe then you'll understand
what I expect from us
and you'll tell me the same
and we'll move from lust
to something a little closer to love

## I killed a spider

I watched it crawl up my wall
and stuck a tissue to its tomb
until it left a slight brown mark
that haunts my white walls
with the reminder that I hurt
just because I was told to hurt

so I wonder if you saw me the same
as a lone spider crawling towards you
and instead of letting me go gently
you stamped my love against your chest
and laid me to rest in the cemetery
of all the girls who you have hurt
just because you was hurt before

I remember that day
we were in the kitchen
and I passed you a half opened can
asking you to do the rest

you did your best
but tore your skin
in the process

and I noticed the issue
so I grabbed as many tissues
as I could because I knew
you were allergic to plasters

I remember the blood running so fast
I never thought it would stop bleeding
but instead of worrying, you just laughed
and said you didn't feel it at all

so I laughed too
I laughed with you

and after an hour or two
the wound closed
but stayed permanently

I'd see the deep scar on your finger
months after the incident
and I'd always trace my thumb over it
an intimate reminder that I was there

it is strange now that I can no longer do that

it is strange that a piece of us
is marked upon your body
like a tattoo full of memory

I wonder if you remember me

when you look down at your finger
does the moment linger
or is it merely a cut
the memory shut
with nothing more to it

I wonder what you'll tell the next girl
who will ask how you got it
would you tell her that it happened
in my dad's kitchen

would she listen as you told her
we went home that evening
and I kissed the pain away
that you stayed over
that we melted into each other
that we could have been mistaken for one body

or would you tell her
that you're sorry
and that you simply
just forgot the story

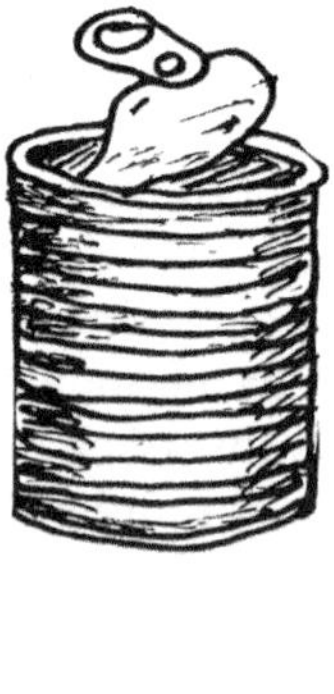

after years of the dust settling
and love becoming dormant
the notion of no-contact becomes unsettling

we could walk past one another
staring at anything but the body
whose soul used to complete the other

we would rather bite our tongues
than exchange syllables that tread
on the rules of a no-contact ending

but you used to hold my heart
until it became overgrown
and it isn't everyday that I find home
in ripping an organ from my ribs
and letting another hold it

it is not every day I choose to love
another like I chose to love you

and though that love has been laid to rest
I know you still visit the cemetery as much as I do
laying flowers in the form of a digital like
whilst I find bouquets in the stems of my ink
and we think the other does not notice

and I know that neither of us
wants to dig up the tomb
for there is no room for dirt and hurt
and the past that would crawl into our skin
there is nothing left for us to love
but does that truly mean that what is left
is a life full of absolutely nothing
to do with one another again?

how can we go from being
the other's entire universe
to nothing but a mere atom
of something long ago?

how do we not bleed nostalgia
at the fact we will go to our graves
never uttering a single word again?

the break up felt more real
when everyone knew

pictures deleted
no feed with me and you

six years of forever
ended when no one saw us together

and that's the moment
the questions came through

and I couldn't answer without crying
it wasn't that I was lying
but I couldn't physically speak
without the words making me feel weak

because when I'd say we broke up
it would break me into pieces
my heart would smash
and I'd have to pretend I didn't feel it

but I did, intensely
and I missed you immensely
and I'd have to look at you
knowing you'd never look at me the same
I'd have to answer questions
and go through the pain
over and over and over again

I wonder if you also had to do the same

how can love end up like that
so thick with resentment
that you've forgotten the contentment
that used to run through the start

now you're breaking apart
holding each other's hearts
not because you want to
but because you're stuck

and fuck am I nothing but a lover
but all I feel is the other
pulling away and away
*please can you stay*
I say, but you've already left

it doesn't matter if you're here
this isn't life, it's our death

we are just waiting, hesitating
sitting in a prison of pretend

are you going to do it first?
are you ready for the end?

I am not going to beg
to mean something to you

it was never a break up
yet my heart screamed as if it were
it tore itself into little lifetimes
wondering why I wasn't her

I'm embarrassed to bleed raindrops
over someone not worth the spill

I hold my insides as they twist into knots
and I wonder whether you will

ever fall for me in the way that I have
or whether we will drift into past tense

you told me you knew you wanted me
I don't think you ever knew what you meant

I let glass bleed under my fingernails
as I grip the remaining parts of my heart
and beg the world for something, *anything*

to let me forget you

you have consumed my existence
ever since you walked into my life
and decided upon your impact

you leave
you return
you leave
you return

and I still haven't learnt
how to let you go

to be an almost
and never a definite
is one of love's biggest cruelties

I am always on the cusp
of being enough
for a man who cannot admit he loves me
or trusts me
or even lusts for me

until he realises I am suddenly
pulling away
then he will say
everything I want to hear
and these fears they disappear

and I fall for it, again

because if I pretend enough
then maybe he will finally admit
he loves me
or trusts me
or even lusts for me

when someone asks why it ended
I say it just wasn't meant to be

but truly it felt like my heart
clawed at the bone in my chest
that you tore me limb from limb
until there was nothing left
but a shadow of who I used to be

you were too focused
on what you couldn't be
that you didn't realise
I'd love you for who you were

and I suppose that's what hurts most

I'd love you in all the lifetimes
but you couldn't even love me in this one

I made you a better man

or rather
the way you tore me into two
somehow became the glue
to put you back together

it took breaking me apart
for you to be able to promise
somebody else forever

*and I never saw it coming*

this person you are becoming
is someone who I begged you to be

why do they always change
for the other woman?

<u>why do they never change
for me?</u>

I could have fallen in love with you
broken every piece of me to fix us

I would have watched you do it too
and yet it would never have been enough

we were never meant to love
only to yearn at our romantic resistance

and feel that we must love
from just a platonic distance

I don't know where we stand
on one hand, it is like nothing has changed
the pictures are still there, the world is still the same
but the scent of you lingers in my bed
and the words you said spin me into confusion
I don't like this allusion to a life together
or a platonic forever that is full of what if's

*why did we ever complicate us?*

falling into temptation
was the worst decision
we ever made

and so I wonder whether Eve was disappointed
when her teeth sunk into the apple's core
did she watch the spell of temptation fall
revealing what was always there before

just a mere piece of fruit
tasting of something
that meant absolutely nothing
and ruined everything to her core

in two years
you will forget me
and I don’t know
why that doesn’t scare me

I told you how hard it was for me to let you in

yet you stroked the softness of my cheeks
whispering everything my heart yearned for
watching the way my eyes twinkled even when
I swore it would take time for me to love again

but you knew I could never resist trying to fix you

so you took hours to respond
claiming love letters take time
but you only ever spoke of your day
barely asking about mine
and though you kissed me like the sunrise
you barely stayed through the mornings
for you preferred tequila to tea
you preferred my body to loving me

and still I let you stay

I opened every door because you swore
that with time you will be what I need
and I held on, the rope of your love
burning the softness of my skin
yet you held me like an oath, smiled like a prayer
and begged for me to believe
only to leave once it got too close to love

I gave my all to you
but it was never enough

loving you is like marvelling
the sunrise for the last time

it once meant everything to us

it always comes around
its presence crafted like clockwork
and yet its beauty still seems so rare

and I know that when it stops
I'll have to go on pretending
like something fundamental didn't just happen

that I'll have to ignore the sunset coming around
all seductive and soothing
as the long night starts to emerge
bleakness draped in an abyss of nothingness

loneliness.

simply a moon full of memories and nothing more

two brief moments
in a day of mundane distraction

this is happening quite fast
will this passion last
or merely decline
will you be mine
or just another number on a list
of the people I have kissed
and missed out on ever truly knowing

should it take a lifetime to love someone?

is learning how to love
the way to find security
in a world full of chaos

shouldn't I just fall?

maybe it is reckless
and wildly impulsive
but surely then you know
whether their ground
will hold you

I think I am searching for love
to escape the person I have become

if someone chooses to fall
then perhaps I wont feel as small
as the world keeps telling me I am

## go back to him

let him walk back into your arms
and then trample over your body
crushing your ribs, heart and hope
before he even says hello

oh but when he does it'll be worth it

the inconsistencies and ambiguities
will lead to a lousy *I love you*
that will be buried underneath
the effort he doesn't want to give you

but go back to him
at least you know
he'll never give you anything more

I dream of you often

as though my subconscious
clings to the closure it creates
in the absence of what you never gave me

I imagine finding home
in each other's laughter again
listening to our favourite song
as the world's judgement falls away

*I can't listen to that song anymore*

I cannot go down the roads
that hold the memory of you
for it is not simply concrete anymore
but a cemetery of everything
we will never be again

*we will never be again*
and it sinks deep into my core
I know I'll find love again
but it can't be yours anymore

you changed the way my heart can beat

I am now a lover girl wrapped in caution
a crime scene that hopes to heal
I now love with uncertainty
but I never used to wait to feel

and I think what hurts more
than the pain of when you left
is how my heart cannot love
or take an innocent breath

I am different now
I am damaged
I am broken
I am healing

I am changed

you hurt me
after promising you wouldn't

and I know I shouldn't
think about it
but I do

my mind wanders
and all roads lead to you
and everything that was never said

I'm now alone
left to roam
in the cycles of my head
you made this bed
and now I lie in it

I ask myself why is it
so hard to leave the past behind
I ask myself how
I can hurt so intensely
when you seem just fine

this love is not a trial run
I am not a sample to taste
you cannot throw my heart out
*I will not be your waste*

I cannot help but hesitate
like a heart afraid to beat
so I'm flying without wings
and I'm running without feet

until the ground soaks my soul
I am resisting the soft sentimental
still the dirt whispers into my core
*you have made me centre-mental*

his lips did not taste like yours
his touch was far softer
his gaze rested upon my eyes
for just that little bit longer

and though I thought of you
I thought of him a lot more
and so I am glad that his lips
tasted different from yours

I let you play me like a fool

you pulled out a deck of cards
and told me the rules
claiming I'd learn them soon enough
you'd begin to show me lust
and convince me it was love

I believed your words
I thought that if I heard
what I wanted to hear
then maybe your fear
of commitment would disappear

but it didn't
it never seemed to stop
you'd never tell me what we were
only what we were not

I still thought you'd learn to love
if I just gave it my all
but you gave me nothing
except a place to brace a fall

and when we reached the ending
your apology came through
you told me I was better off
without confining myself to you
and though my heart hurt
and my body curled into its core
I realised I no longer wanted to stay
and I finally shut the door

I think I'll miss your family more than you

the laughter filling up pints around your uncle's makeshift bar; different souls but the soles of our feet not sitting very far. huddling together, no matter whether we've met briefly, or discreetly.

and your dad really liked me

he'd whisper gratitude, say something slightly rude about the way you were before. he'd tell me I was more than what you've known. he'd tell me that he hopes you've finally grown up. but no matter being the *best girl you knew*, your dad understood I was too good for you.

you did too.

but it didn't stop me from staying or playing myself into our loss. I cost myself a heart tearing from caring about whether you were on your phone. I'd convince myself you were busy when you told me you'd be home. and I'd hear your dad's voice saying you'd finally grown but I knew that commitment was something you've never truly known.

but I thought I could fix you; I thought the issue was the lack of attempt. I thought it meant that I would be the one to change you, to rearrange you into the perfect shape of who I wanted you to be. I realise now that that wasn't healthy for you nor was it healthy for me.

we were made to break for both of us to see that you had growing to do and I had loving to see.

I was not made for casual love

for one night stands
and drunken kisses
I'm the type of girl
who looks at stars and wishes
I was not made for liking stories
and waiting for their texts
I was not made for situationships
or moving onto the next
for I was born with a heart
that beats in the tune of sunsets
I may have born to forgive
but I wasn't made to forget
if you tell me your favourite songs
there will be a playlist where they're stored
and if you tell me of your passions
then I shall never be bored
because I love with intention
and I kiss you with a promise
I'd pour my energy into you
and I'd always be honest
I've never struggled to commit
because I know the way in which I love
and for the right person, I am certain
that this will always be enough

you tore me apart so brutally
that I thought I was the only person
to have ever hurt so badly
from a broken heart

and then I realised

I was one piece in a mosaic
of the heartbroken

there were many before us
and there will be more of us
and there was comfort in the fact

that we won't ever be alone

growing - a definition of poetry

this chapter follows the whirlwind of being a first year at university.

it contains the excitement, the spontaneity, the disappointment, the stagnancy, the loneliness, the chaos, the love, the loss, the distance, the yearning, the acceptance and the gratitude.

as a child I struggled to even sleep over at a friend's house for the night without my Mum there but as an adult I chose to move three hours away from the only place I've ever known. as an adult I fell in love with the independence, the laughter, the anarchy, the subsequent stability, the environment and the people. as an adult I fell in love with the way I opened myself up to something I used to think was impossible for me to do. as an adult university became the place where I finally settled into my skin.

but this chapter also acknowledges its own limits.

university is not a one-size-fits-all experience. it varies depending on who you are and where you are. it varies upon whether you live at home or in halls, on your flatmates, your degree, your campus, your friends, your course-mates (there is a difference between the two), your confidence, your interests, and a myriad more factors that could fill up all the pages of this book if I continued to list them.

but that is all part of *growing out*, right?

# Growing Out

four walls, a bathroom and
a kitchen shared between strangers

*would I survive this?*

emptiness swiftly lights the halls
we smile politely and pass each other by

*should I survive this?*

a night out, a few drinks
we start to share secrets softly

*could I survive this?*

new faces beam on my walls
and the room feels softer now

*I might survive this*

plates pile up, arguments rise
but our doors start to open wider

*I want to survive this*

and suddenly I've found family
in people I never knew a year ago

*so I think we will survive this*

open doors, campus stretching
this is the time to be alive

everyone is smiling
everyone is alone
everyone is changing

so you make a few friends
you walk, you talk, you go back home
you may text occasionally
if they have your number in their phone

and it's hard
because finding your people
doesn't happen overnight
but it feels like it should
so these friends hover

they smile

they run

they sit

they float

they stay

they go

they return

they drink

they laugh

they leave

they smile

but it feels like
they were never really there
just brief moments
in a span of unspoken loneliness

at first everything is identical

the trees are all green
and the buildings are all tall
and there you are, walking
wondering if this is all there is

but time cleans the seasons away
and suddenly life changes

the trees are like soft arrows
guiding you towards the grey building
and there you are, striding
into the doors of your lecture hall

and you realise that you
knew exactly where
you were going all along

we have tore each other into pieces
and made peace over shared bowls
of freshers fair ramen noodles

we have had plates rise to the ceiling
and walls peeling with nights
we can barely remember

we have had keys gone missing
and pictures of kissing strangers
just sitting above the bin

we have had dinners on the table
where we able to let go of the world
for just one more moment

yes, this kitchen is far from perfect
but it is all worth it because
at least for one year it was *ours*

there were group chats upon group chats
Facebook, Instagram, WhatsApp
and I joined them all

I narrowed it down to accommodation
accepted every friend request invitation
to find the people in my hall

I found one, then we ended up with another
we made a group chat with each other
and then soon we moved in

I didn't know what to expect
but I'll never forget
how it felt to simply begin

hangovers used to be fun

hands were sticky from sweets
not sweat, sex and shots
headaches were from laughter
not deafening DJ tracks
that aren't actually very good

waking up consisted of bin bags
stuffed to the brim with pillows
and pink princess blankets
not the clinking of empty bottles
that no one remembers buying

the morning debrief of dreams
turned into the morning debrief of
*what the fuck did I do?*

the promises of *let's do it again,*
*do not forget!* turned into
*we can't drink again, there's*
*too much I regret*

sleepovers lost their innocence
and in a sense
the car rides home did too

and suddenly nothing was
ever like it used to be
hangovers used to be fun
*what on earth happened to me?*

I am planting seeds in a minefield

watering plants
I know the bomb of time
will soon displace

my roots here
will not flourish
they will simply erase

but here I am
finding foundations
despite the truth

that soon we will leave
and be left to grieve
the place that defined our youth

I know these moments will end
I won't pretend
that my place here is forever
I know we won't be together
for all of our lives
but just because I recognise
that university has an expiration
does not mean this is an invitation
for our golden moments to pass

*I really hope these days will last*

sometimes all you want is your mum
after all that has been said and done
you just want her to tuck you into bed
stroke the hair upon your head
and tell you it will all be okay

but you've wished her away too soon
and you wake up in a strangely familiar room
with a headache and a hangover
wishing she would come over
but now she lives 140 miles away

*journal entry #1*

never in my life have I felt that protected by a group of girls I haven't even properly met before. such kindness, tenderness, softness; divine feminine energy that often is too superficial to come by anymore. there were three girls; one a beacon of light, one a beacon of hope and the other was a beacon that would always guide you home. yesterday I could not recall their faces, today I could tell you all that they hope to be.

I can feel you slipping

after all, isn't that
what distance does?

a sunrise is always
separated from the sea

so I wonder if it
will always be

only ever you
and only ever me

a mathematical system
jumbles up souls and
distributes them in patterns
so random it seems almost fated

these lives are interwoven
from the click of a button
and suddenly you couldn't imagine
not eating dinner with these numbers

- *an ode to the system that led to us being flatmates*

we are all on a budget

whether it be
financial or emotional
social or societal

we are all trying to find balance
in a world that demands
us to know the form of value
and be ready to sacrifice it
in the hopes of being responsible

I am not who I was when I left home

these four walls
and first year halls
have altered who I am

I am no longer a shadow
haunting a hometown
I've since overgrown
but now finally someone whole

I have made a home here

a year ago these faces
were simply strangers
but now I couldn't imagine
a life without their smiles

yet in a few days I will leave
and find myself haunting
the house I can no longer call home

I know I'll have to pack my bags soon

take down the photos and the club tickets and the polaroids and the receipts and the cards that lined my bedroom wall. hang them in a room that no longer reflects this chapter of my life.

I know I'll have to pack my bags soon

take out the plates and the cutlery and the toothpicks and the cookbooks and the photos that lined our kitchen wall. store them in a cupboard that suffocates the memories they hold in whispers

I know I'll have to pack my bags soon

take them home but it isn't home when you've roamed far enough to find home in halls and faces, in walls and spaces that started out strange but feel more familiar than the house you grew up in.

I know I'll have to pack my bags soon
but I really wish I didn't have to

and somehow you're at the end of first year

the days of lost wandering
seem so lost in the fog of the past
and now you're walking through sunsets
with friendships that *did* last

and you don't even want to go home

that little room that was empty
is now full of the person you've become
you have planted your roots here
you have soaked up the sun

this chapter is about the complexity of family.

the unconditional love that beats from a heart they created for you. the subsequent tearing of that same heart the more you grow. the ache for them to put it back together again. the ache for the innocence of childhood. the ache of ignorance before you learnt the truth of family. the ache of knowing they do not know much more than you.

the aching, the aching, the aching.

it is also the gratitude that you have for the sacrifices your grandparents made. the gratitude that you have for your mother's courage when she raised two children as a single parent. the gratitude that you have for your older sister when she finally put herself first. the gratitude that you have for the lessons of unwavering strength. the gratitude that you have for all of the laughter.

the gratitude, the gratitude, the gratitude.

it is also about learning what parts of you remain tied to those roots and what parts become severed. it is about learning who you are beyond what you have always known. it is about learning you do not have to stay that way forever.

but that's all part of knowing where you are *growing from*, right?

# Growing From

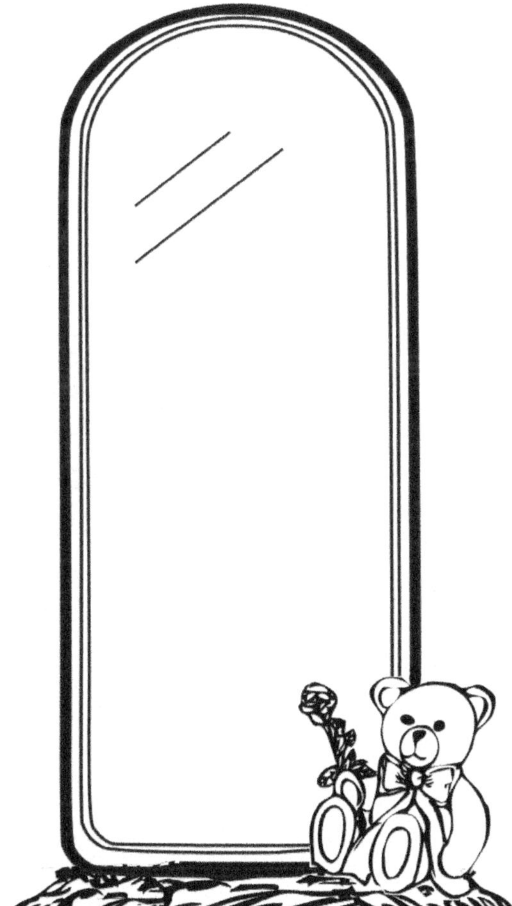

genetics code our existence
predisposing us to a lifetime of imitation

we attempt to escape the fate
that is bestowed upon us
but it often proves too late

we are the mirrors of our ancestors
dooming those who haven't even learnt
how to take a breath yet

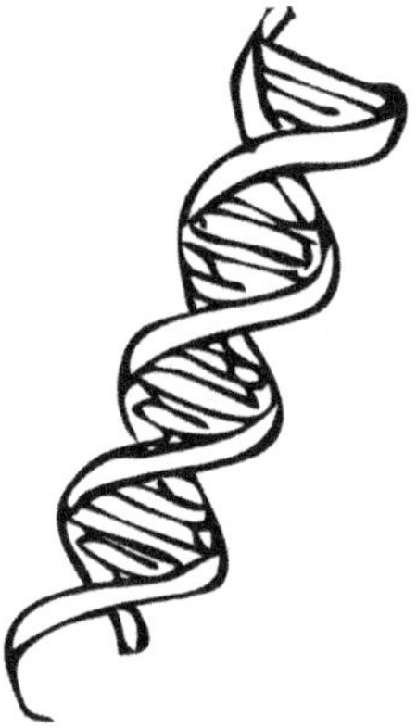

the moment your parents
are revealed to be people
is the moment when life seems to shift

you are now seen to exist
because the childhood lens
that blurred your sight is falling

and you cannot
keep
stalling
growing up

because it is here

you are not warned
to fear this moment

but you can feel
the years burning

and you are now yearning
for the simplicity of
innocence

in a sense
this is when your life
has truly begun
and although you are young
you now carry an
expectation of purpose

and if you do not know
your destination
you slip into being
worthless

I realise I resent you
and I know I'm not meant to
but I cannot help it

you don't listen to my silence
and you cannot hear my screams
you never seem to respond
to the nature of your dreams

and it shakes me hollow
because you could have been
absolutely everything I see in you

my mother's sadness
curled up into her genes
sleeping dormant with grief
until it found the relief
of expressing itself in me

- *epigenetics*

I watch a daughter
become the mother
she swore she'd never be

I watched a mother
lose her daughter
and now she passes it to me

I am a daughter
with a mother
who cannot seem to listen

when I am a mother
with a daughter
I promise I'll be different

my nan has always worried
my mother, my sister too
we're a generation of women
we're layers of our blues

we all panic, we all count
we all worry about the end
we all hold each other up
and we always pretend

that this life doesn't scare us
but we are all so afraid
it's woven into our genetics
*fear is how we were made*

it is one of those days where I am rotting in my old bedroom, letting childhood memories fill my lungs with dust, coughing at the truth that I lived here not too long ago.

my hometown is lonely
compared to what it was
the places that meant so much
have crumbled to dust
and I'm left with nostalgia
carved into a cemetery

I cannot hold myself together here

I become undone.

clothes strewn on the floor, my heart cracking
somewhere beneath it all, just unravelling and
unravelling and unravelling.

I can only ever be a mess when I am home.

my childhood home no longer fits me anymore

it is too short, cutting at my calves
and shutting off all the warmth inside me

since I left I have walls that no longer
suffocate the very being of which I am
I have windows that finally let
the sun pour itself through

I am older now

I see myself etched into the creaks of the steps
so I tend to tread a little lighter now
avoiding every crack and crease
that only ever hurt someone

I am stronger now

I can lift the heavy boxes up the stairs
and appreciate that it is still not my burden to bare

I wear who I am with pride

and being inside this place I called home
no longer makes me feel alone
but it is a reminder of where I have been
and how much I have grown

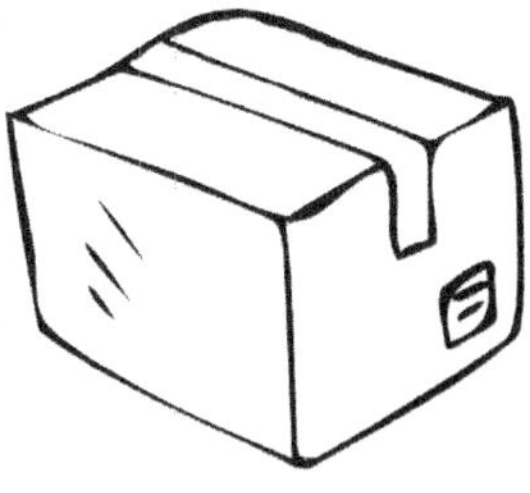

my older sister grew up
as the first child

she made the mistakes
I have learnt from

she healed from the heartbreak
I know not to fall for

she had to be a daughter
without someone telling her
what they expected to see

I am nothing if not the woman
she has taught me to be

## an ode to the older siblings

you grew up before you
grew into the shape of your body
learning how time is quick
to shake your innocence
when you see your sibling
about to stand in the same trauma
that nobody protected you from
and instead you pick up every shard
and let it bleed your heart open
before it ever scratches theirs

we share half a DNA
but I know nothing of the way
that shapes the person you've become

I do not envy the nuclear family
I simply wonder what it is like
to grow up with two parents
who live in their love for one another

*my mother was also my father*

though he was often present
he was never exactly there
so again she had to give up spare
parts of herself to make me whole

*my mother was also my father*

though he made me laugh
he was never there when I cried
but my mother knew my favourite song
and wiped my tears to its tune

*my mother was also my father*

though he showed me how to defend
my thumb above my fingers in a fist
my mother taught me how to fight back
with her wit and dangerous defiance

*my mother was also my father*

though he nodded at the stories
I would tell about adolescent antics
my mother knew their names and
could tell you who was truly meant for me

*my mother was also my father*

though he was a father too
distance did limit what he could do
and my mother made sure I never
had to worry about filling in that gap

I never thought I came from a broken home

perhaps my parents weren't together
and my siblings were a little complicated
but even my six year old self knew
that sometimes life isn't convenient

*if they are happier apart*
*that's all that matters*
I used to tell myself

and it's not like they ended badly

but as their hearts broke
pieces of that glass shattered
the moments of my future
that were supposed to be whole

my graduation
my wedding
and all the other moments
that will now be fractured
by a home that only now feels broken

I used to imagine us on Christmas day

two people
stemmed from broken families
loving each other enough
to make their own home whole

we'd have the Christmas
we never had as children

but then you left
and I was left wondering
how on earth we tried
to be something that always
fought against us in our blood

I promise to build a house of love

where amber hues kiss the pictures
that line every edge of our walls

it will be a haven of music
with laughter that outshines an orchestra
where shouts only escape from lips
when UNO gets too competitive
and hearts break because of life
not because of each other

I promise to build a house of sunsets

where we bask in the afterglow
of a day well spent together
and we build pillow forts at midnight
tasting smores and sweets
and not being scared to ask for another

I promise to build a home for you

the negativity of my old home
clings to its walls like dust

it spits out cruelty on command
as if it were wired to be unkind

written in flattened braille
are rules you must know
in order to merely exist

break one and watch the floors
shake with irrational rage
so accept it and promise to be better

*I promise to be better*

I press the fabric to my nose
and breathe you in
waiting for the scent
of your cigarettes
to bring me home

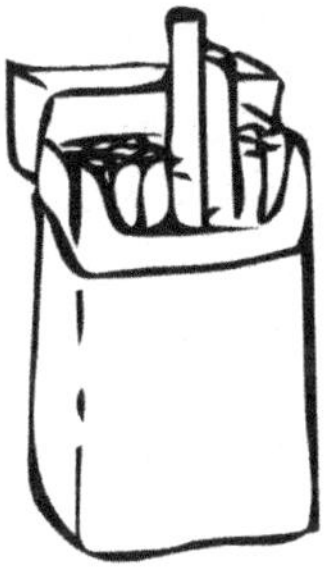

all the screaming
and the sadness
are tuned out against
the sound of this moment

our happiness is *musical*

it is the type of joy
that even the butterflies
in my stomach giggle along to

it has the same chords
and first fret belly laughter
that filled the soundtrack of my childhood

I am nostalgic

for soaring on park swings. for the
seconds of unity over fish finger
Happy Meals. for the thrill of my
face painted in the perfect shade of
unicorn. for the magic contained in snow.
for my first calligraphy pen. for stumbling
around the house in my sister's stilettos. for
the brief moment of flight when they shouted
*1-2-3* and swung me in the air. for the sleepovers. for the
midnight snacks. for hoping I'd reach the ice cream man
in time. for hoping. for not knowing that my parents
were people. for not knowing it was their first time here
too. for not knowing that I cannot change what broke
them. for not knowing that what broke them will break
me too.

for not knowing
anything but
the sound of this moment

I'm not strong enough for this anymore

my younger self
with her untameable fire
would burn and burn and burn
the minute you made her cold

now I simply shiver

I bite my tongue
hoping the blood
will choke my anger

I'm not made for this war anymore

I feel like I've coloured myself
outside of the lines

I can hear them shouting
that I'm incomplete and
excessive simultaneously

I can hear them whispering
that I'll never be enough

but I have poured
hours into healing
and I'm exhausted of seeing
insecurity overgrown

I'm tired of trying to prove
that I can stay in between your lines
when I struggle to stay in mine

you tell me it's cold

and so I find some wood
and light your personal sun
for you to complain that it burns

*will I ever be good enough for you?*

this chapter holds the pain that tends to consume us.

it carries the anxieties, the depression, the insecurities, the body dysmorphia, the OCD, the disassociation, the dread, the fear, the anger and the pleading to be 'normal'. the poems within this chapter explore these topics quite briefly, poetically dipping in and out of each focus, but I felt it necessary to divulge a little further into one more specifically.

in the past few years of my life, I was consumed by the notion of health anxiety. the panic attacks were relentless, the fear was prevalent and the thoughts were terrifying. I truly thought I was the only person to have ever felt such fear. I'd lose nights convincing myself that I wasn't okay. I'd lose days feeling guilty for the way my thoughts worked when I was grateful to be perfectly well. I'd lose weeks within this cycle. I'd lose myself.

at some point within our lives, we lose ourselves to something that pains us. often when it is not physical, we choose to either neglect it or invalidate it purely because it cannot be covered by a plaster. this chapter serves to remind you that pain, whether it be physical or mental, hurts and that hurt deserves to be heard, seen and treated for the pain that it caused you.

you deserve to be seen for everything you've been *growing through*, right?

# Growing Through

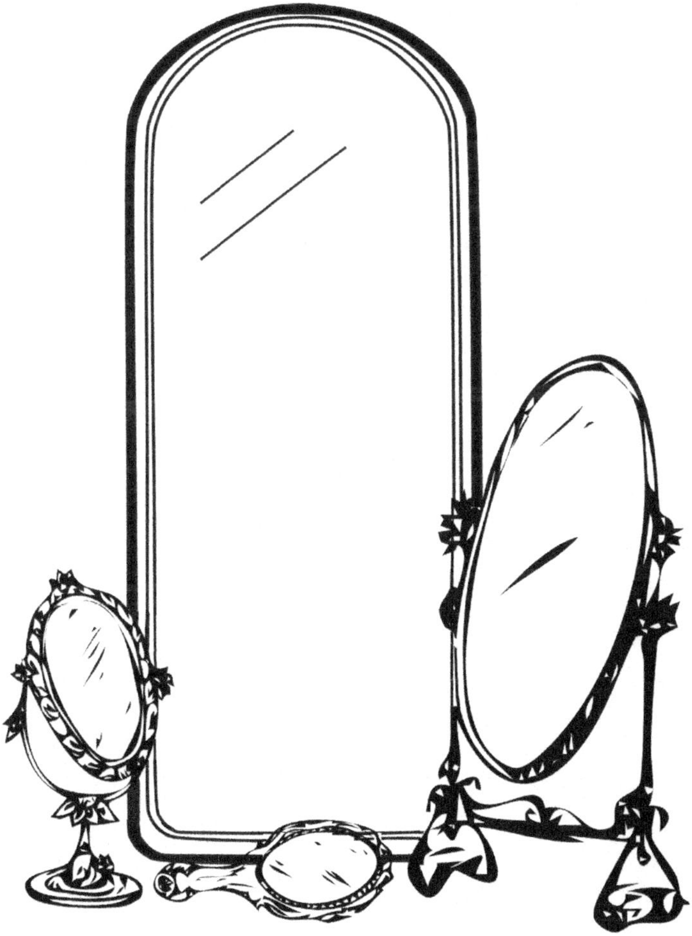

a list of things I have outgrown…

skinny jeans
lip balm that tastes like soda
2010 Instagram photo filters
the girl I thought would be my bridesmaid
red converses
oversized scrunchies
the man I spent six years loving
finding my childhood DS
the need to laugh at a joke that isn't funny
the fear of taking medication
getting the friendship group back together
the morning routine of standing on scales
asking for the bare minimum
skinny jeans

what's this age
if not a plague
upon the teenage girls

my ten-year-old self
so desperately wanted to be thin
because at least then
she would be accepted

and that was worth
so much more
than being happy

how sad that the earth
has circled the sun
for another decade
and still nothing has changed

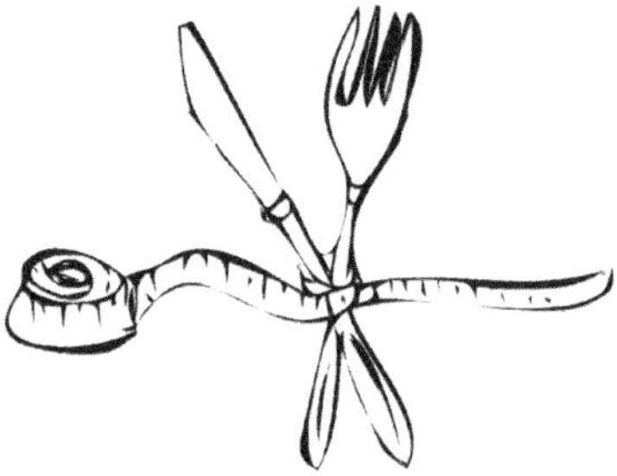

I do not know what I anticipate
all I know is that I am waiting

and it is frustrating
to not see clearer
to not face the mirror
and see my purpose
intertwined within my reflection

I stare at imperfection
without a detection of a clue
about who I want to be
or what I want to do

I have never had sex
that made me mindless enough
to forget about how I look

*I have never been comfortable*

as puzzle pieces slot together
I feel as though my corners are worn
and that I could never make
this as picture perfect as it should be

*I have never been comfortable*

I'll attempt to keep my clothes on
and give as much to them as I can
before I ever let them simply see me
or hold me, or taste me, or want me

*I have never been comfortable*

but I hope one day I will be

I don't want to tell you my flaws
not because I don't trust you
but I know your eyes
will realise them more
when I say I'm insecure

you will see them
you will see *me*
and everything I'm scared I'll always be

and honestly
I can't having you knowing
I can't have me showing
the parts of me I despise

I can't have you realise
that at my core
I am so incredibly insecure

I sit in my sorrow
I compare unmade tomorrows
and make my bed
until the sun sets
and I start again

I do not eat
even if every thought
sounds like food
until I wash my hair
with strands clinging
to my bony fingers
and I start again

I panic in secret
feeling the fear stick
to my cells in worry
until everything goes numb
and I start again

I write in patterns
this poetry an attempt
to glamorise the darkest parts
of the self that I am
until I stop typing
and am left with everything
I have tried not to be
and I start again

I choke on the mirror

its glass lodges itself
into the gaps of my throat
and slices my senses
until I am left defenceless
to an insistent insecurity

and I can't scream anymore
because the shards have ripped
my tongue into tangles of truths
that I will never be good enough

*will I ever be good enough?*

I try and remind myself
that being skinny
has never solved my mind

I still find myself
longing to be thin
even when bone
is leaking out of skin
even when my hair
is pulled from my scalp
even when I loose myself
an extreme amount

it didn't solve a thing

yet I sit here wondering
whether this time it could
whether I should let myself fall
back into my trembling arms again

I wish my weight did not define my childhood
like a harsh underline on a poem

I wish the reason I was bullied
was because I liked to sing a lot

I wish a boy called me beautiful
before I taught myself to be thin

I wish I did not look so
obviously different in the old pictures

I wish they did not tell me I look so
obviously different in the old pictures

I wish I wasn't proud that I look so
obviously different in the new pictures

I wish I did not wish that I look
obviously different in the new pictures

I wish I did not wish that I look

different.

I can feel the release of hunger
burning guilt in my stomach
and pounding thoughts in my mind
that scream how I should have
held off on eating for a little longer

I can feel the ache of flavour
crawling down my throat
scraping my tongue
until it finds the same out
that it did when it came in

I can feel my skin throb
as it increases in simply seconds
filling the room with flesh
until the mirror is shattered
at the mere sight of me

sometimes I still feel
as though I am nine years old
gazing into the mirror
wondering when I'll grow into myself

things I'm still learning to love…

the way my body sits in clothing
the taste of raw fish on sushi
the lessons in letting them go
the beauty in thunder and lightening
wide-leg jeans
the sound of my laughter in videos
leaving my childhood behind
the passing of time
my sensitivity to being loved
the way my body sits in clothing
my body in clothing
my body.

a list of who I am…

my favourite colour is pink
I'm allergic to strawberries
I wish I continued musical theatre
I miss everyone I've ever loved
I fear taking medication
my grades define my worth
I think about my body 24/7
reading allows me to escape my thoughts
the smell of cigarettes reminds me of home
the concept of no-contact unnerves me
I think about an ex-friend often
the stars make me feel safe
the inevitability of death terrifies me
I am grateful to be alive
I love love more than anything else
I feel unlovable
spring is my favourite season

there has to be a world
that describes the physical feeling
of insecurity tearing into my skin

it is a type of burning
that leaves me learning
of the deep cold within

and it should be alarming
that I am accustomed to a touch
that knows how to squeeze me thin

I am reduced to everything
that I never wanted to be
*when does self love begin?*

today I've decided I don't like my chin

of all the list of insecurities
I'm sure this niche will fit in

I don't like the way it sits
or the way it fits
around my face
taking up space
like it's meant to be there

tomorrow I'll decide I don't like my thighs

that my desired curves
are deserved to be despised

I don't like the way they fall
the fact they're not small
and that they have more skin
I wish that they were slim
like they are meant to be

next week I'll decide I don't like my nose

the way it seems too small
it can't be right, I suppose

I don't like the way it lifts
maybe I could pay to have it shift
but it's expensive to pay
and I don't know if I'd like the way
it is 'meant' to be

maybe my body is
just meant for me

if only it were hearts in a notebook
not gut-wrenching poetry

if only it were getting ready
because I wish that he would notice me

if only it were doodles on the skin
not scars from a blade

if only it was because I didn't
like the food I had made

I don't want to
love like I'm losing
or live like
I'm choosing

between optimism
and pessimism
into silence
and petty rhythms

I don't want to be torn
between dying and surviving
I want to live life
without realising

that one day I won't
but it sinks to my core
I'm too scared to die
but I can't take it anymore

every night
the moon
gets a
little brighter

but every time
my heart
braves
another fight

I'm tired

but I don't want to go to sleep
because my fear of death
is the biggest secret that I keep

on a good day
I can control my breathing

inhale, exhale
and watch the thoughts float
away into the stream
of a deeper consciousness

but other days
I become a puppet
dancing to the fear
of my mere existence

exhale
  inhale
      pant
        five senses
            check pulse

inhale, exhale
you find yourself back

*you've survived this*
my heart sings
*this time is different*
my mind laughs

and suddenly my lungs
cannot tell whether they are
breathing to survive
or breathing to deceive

I inhale, I exhale
but I cannot breathe

it’s like someone holds you
in the sharp grip of their fist
they spin your eyes around
you don’t believe you exist
and the ground is unfamiliar
but you walk it just the same
you dissociate from life
you don’t understand your name
and they tell you it’ll pass
but what does that even mean
if you start to panic at the thought
that life is just a dream
and you cannot wake up
but if you do you won’t know
dissociate, disassociate
but I just can’t let go

it's not never been just a headache
or chest pain, or shortness of breath
it's the epitome of the end
*am I closer to death?*

no, the doctors are wrong
no, do another test
yes, I know I am wrong
yes, I'm trying my best

but I'm so incredibly scared
of the day I'll see the light
that I'll convince myself I'm dying
that something isn't right

and I know how it sounds
and I'm grateful just to be
but I miss when I used to live
without this side of me

it felt like my body was screaming

that every nerve cell was hurting
and every bone was breaking
and every organ was failing

it felt like the worst had come

that every moment was fleeting
that every second was losing
that everything would just stop

but it didn't

the clouds cleared
and my fear was just that

<u>fear</u>

I ruin the moment with nostalgia

it's dangerous

it slices through happiness
lodging itself between my ribs
beating me to burst open

my heart gets jealous
as it squeezes my lungs
between its tiny fingers

*breathe*
    *breathe*
        *breathe*

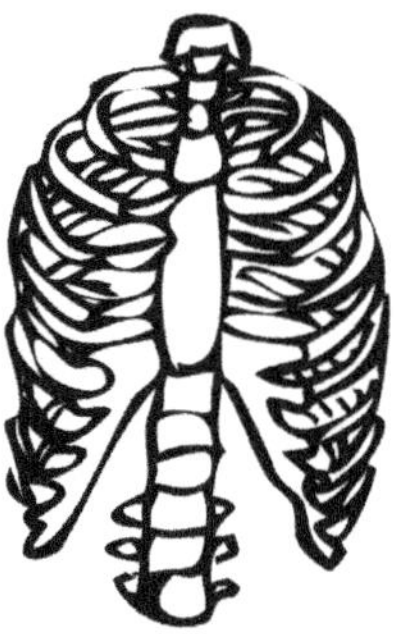

I'm taunted by time

it laughs at me
for everything I was
and will never be again

it cries with me
for everything it took
and will never return

it hopes with me
for everything it is
and cannot understand

but mostly it exists with me
for everything I do
and will cease to do again

my leg begins to beat like a heartbeat
drumming fear into the ground
I search for security and meaning
but there is nothing to be found

and my hands create a melody
upon invisible piano keys
I play and I play and I play
but no one seems to hear me

and I used to find foundations
in the softness of your touch
you used to calm my climbing cries
*oh I miss you very much*

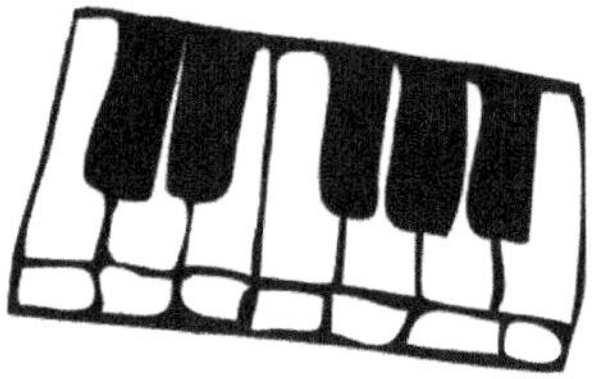

my heart is aching
and shaking my whole being
into a numb explosion of

*everything and nothing*

I feel everything in my stomach
and nothing in its truth
I am watching innocence disappear
and losing a handle on my youth

I am holding myself together
as the world rips me apart
the pills aren't working
I feel the hurting
that is lurking
within my heart

I'm floating

a cloud suspended
waiting to cry
at the slightest moment

but I don't want you to watch me pour

so I hold myself in
watching a storm brew
into thunder
waiting to go under

just waiting
floating

walk on the carpet four times
then you can exhale your breath
you have completed the task
you saved your mother from death

touch the table four times
twice with each hand
do this to save yourself
even if no one understands

do it again and again
because you don't want them to die
you know it is irrational
but you don't know why

you cannot break from the cycle
so you do it once more
four times feels incomplete
so do eight if you're unsure

this chapter gives space to the things that make us feel whole.

it is a dedication to what helps wakes us up in the mornings and fall asleep in the evenings. it is a dedication to the individual escapes we have to make this life a little easier.

as an artist, my escape is in the safety of my pen (or sometimes my keyboard). it is my weapon, my heart, my voice, my vision, my shelter, my downfall and my lifeline. I immortalise every love, loss and lesson in the words that I write. I bleed recovery into every rhyme. I hope dreams into every stanza. I continue to write even when it feels like I have nothing left to make beautiful and my goodness, I am so incredibly grateful to have found home in such a passion.

in the last year I also found solace in spirituality.

I used to be one to scoff at crystals, tarot cards and anything remotely spiritual. I used to be extremely sceptical in trusting in something so profound as the universe. yet understanding the power of the law of attraction, divine femininity, the importance of manifestation and the belief that the universe truly knows what is best for me has allowed me to heal from what had made me broken.

this chapter allows you to think of those individual beliefs, escapes, passions and dreams that have helped you to grow. it allows you to remember that they are part of who you are. it allows you to feel whole again.

and that's all part of *growing with*, right?

# Growing With

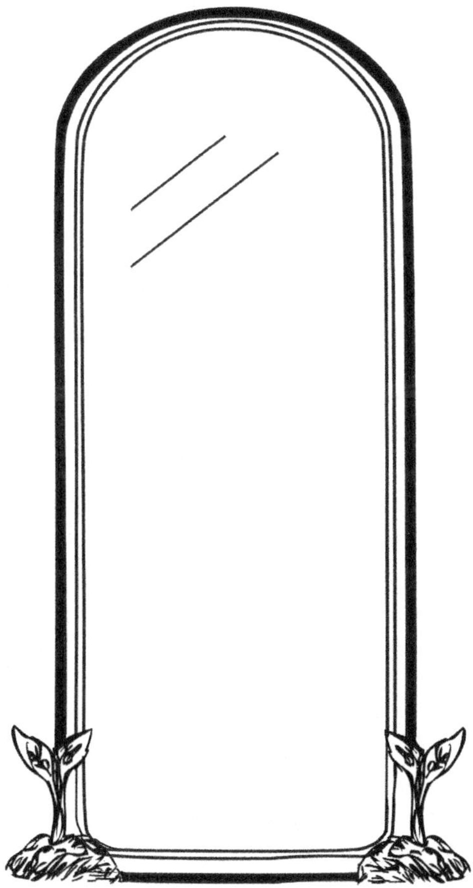

I'd like to be loved enough
to be captured in your art
extend me beyond the confines
of being merely a single part

I want to be the palette
the brushes and the ink
I want my lips to change
the way your eyes can think

I pour myself into these words
hoping to save my light
within the ink of my pages

but what if this print turns to cages
and I am left a forgotten poet
whose words couldn't touch a single heart
whose words only helped to tear her apart

because I am vulnerable when I speak

I immortalise the weakest parts of myself
in hope to find you healing
in the emotions you are feeling

but what if the truth reveals this was futile
and while I have let my blood become ink
no one cares what I think
and I remain the only one to remember
that I never amounted to anything

I fear the ink that flows from my pen

it is dangerous
it is daring

it is way more honest
than I have ever been

I wonder when I'll start writing again

about yesterdays and Tuesdays
and the little life in between
about the large house with maples
and overgrown memory leaves
about lovers and stars and roses
and straightening the back of my hair
about foresight and hindsight
and all the vision I am yet to see
about my mother and my dogs
and the people I have not loved yet

I wonder when I will
immortalise myself
into a single sentence
worth writing about

I wonder when I will
believe I am enough

I loved you so much
that I immortalised you in my words
for you deserved to be loved
in the scrawly notes of my pen

now and then I read over those pages
watch my language shift through the ages
saw the lens change from devotion
to broken hearted emotion

yet still you were there
waving whilst I drowned in my ocean of ink
I think love is overlooked
when expressed in the letters of a book
because there the best parts of you sit forever
regardless if you are still together

you exist no matter where you roam
your existence is still known
even if you are no longer present
surely that is evidence
of loving someone deeply
for by gifting them immortality
they can be remembered completely

describe me, just like I do to you

find the intimate moments
that make the mosaic
of who I am
and paint them

speak me into your existence
just as I write you into mine

love me into your moments
tell them of all our time

the tragedy of art
being appreciated once
the artist has died
says a lot more about humanity
than we care to admit

art transcends time
if anything, art *is* time

because this universe
was created by an artist
who knew their way
around a blank canvas

and though that blooms
into the sun's golden hues
it also manages to lay in our veins
twisting itself around our genetics

art is who we are
art is who we have always been

music has been played
since string touched wood
and there are stories on cave walls
that can still be understood

art is immortal
and I suppose, so are we

manifestation is the perfect blend
between dream and reality

it is the child holding hands
with the mother and finding
a middle ground

it is working in colour

it is learning to balance
passion with time and energy

it is truly believing
that what you desire
is already happening

like a radio, you must
tune into that frequency

and you must *listen*

mercury is about to retrograde

appearing to spin backwards
and unravelling all the energy
I have tried so hard to intertwine

but I suppose if it can be undone
then it was never truly aligned

because what is meant for me
is still destined to be mine

and what is not worth my energy
will be removed from my time

tarot cards flood my feed
and sometimes I truly believe them

I've never been one to understand energy
but sometimes these cards
feel like they're meant for me
my situations are detailed perfectly
it's like their meanings create earth for me
that lay foundations between my feet

I attach the people I meet
to the people the cards describe
and I realise that maybe I was fated to dream

maybe the hurt that seems to never end
is a step closer to befriending
the definition of healing
these cards have me feeling strange sensations

who would have thought a cynic
would use manifestation
but that's exactly what I do

I know many believe them to be untrue
but it doesn't matter to me
whether honest or not
they promise I'm on the way
to where I'm meant to be

### *I don't believe in all that stuff*

the truth is, I'd never ask you to
follow me down a path
that you do not wish to tread

I'd never fill your head
if your heart is unsure
but if you ever wanted to know
then allow me to give a tour

with handfuls of crystals
and a pocket with tarot cards
I sit upon the warmth of the earth
and I simply exist

I let gratitude wash over me
whispering in the wind
and I connect to the ground

the grass lies beneath my toes
the sun kisses my cheek
and I simply exist

I find meaning in the moments
I find truth in the trials
I find home in the honest
I find security in the smiles

and I allow myself
to simply exist

close your eyes
and wait for the hum

feel your body as
its chemicals
start to dance

*you are alive*
*you are breathing*
*you are here*

browse beyond the silence
and tune into the frequency
of your future self

listen to the melody
it's a future memory
encouraging you to connect

to become.

experience is valuable
but our youthful ignorance
tends to ignore the magic
behind an elderly life

they have lived
they have loved
they have lost
they have learnt.

we are mere mortals
in comparison to their eternal life

towards the end of their lifetimes
one tends to share
the foundations to existence
*so why don't we ever listen?*

## what the dead would say to us

go out and choose to laugh
do exactly as you wish
fall in love for a moment
lose yourself in a kiss

feel the sting of love
and forgive all of its pain
trust in someone's smile
and do it all over again

write the novel, sing the tune
immortalise your passion
do not waste your short time
losing your body to a changing fashion

be grateful for all of the seasons
they'll tell you what you need to know
that there are only brief moments to life
turn away and soon it will go

you are as young as you will ever be
and these moments will be past years
breathe in every second of existence
and remember that *you are here*

take five minutes to escape

lose the phone
lose the nicotine
lose the worries

and inhale
to exhale
and inhale
to exhale
and inhale
to exhale

until you forget you were ever trying to escape

this chapter is about the beauty of falling in love.

it's a gallery of all the moments that arrive when you find the person that brings your world into colour. it's a thank-you card for the way they made you believe in love again.

it captures the story of how fate played its part in falling in love with my best friend.

we met each other three years ago at a leadership programme that brought 20 people around the country together. when we met for the first time we clicked almost instantly. we continued to talk once the programme ended (with me in London, him in Manchester). a year and a half later, we both coincidentally end up at the same university. though we were in two separate accommodations (one in which had thousands of students, the other simply hundreds). we had the only two rooms that could see into each other's bedrooms. it felt like fate was smiling at us.

we had always known our connection was strong; everyone around us could feel it and *always* vocalised it from the moment we met. we denied it, unaware of how the other was feeling, claiming that what we had was limited to friendship. but the more time we spent together, the more palpable the energy between us was. denying our feelings for one another was like pulling two magnets apart, trying to resist the nature of physics.

so this chapter is a thank you to the love of my life and the fated story that brought us together. a thank you to the universe for keeping my heart hopeful to believe in a love like this and to the rom-coms that kept me dreaming. a thank you to the way my heart loves.

and that's all part of *growing together*, right?

# Growing Together

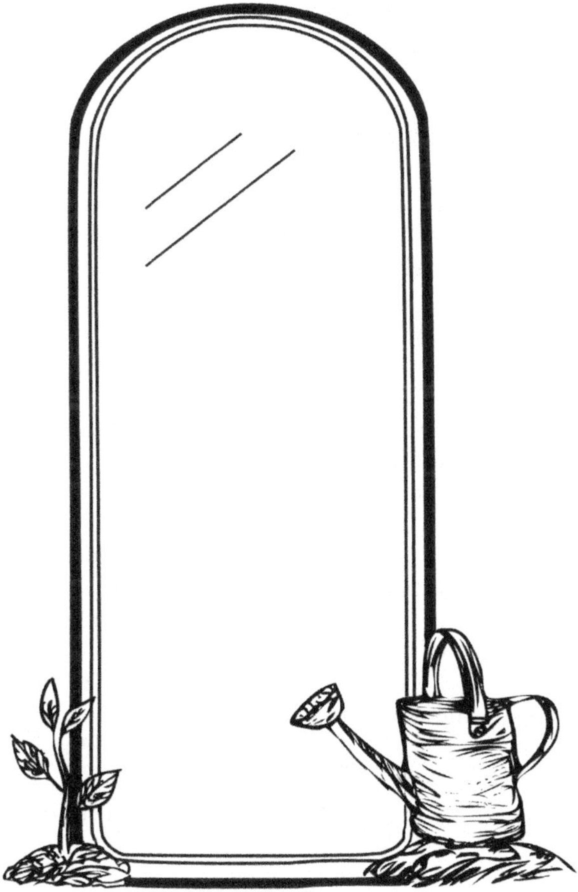

I don't want mediocre love

perhaps he made me feel too much
but I know for someone
my love will be enough for them

it will lift them up
and me in return
we will learn how to love like the poets
and I know it will be true
this mediocre love
I want nothing to do with it
I am completely through with it

I want grand gestures
and simple conversations
I want to hold them when it hurts
and I want to dance at celebrations
I want the rain to soak our hair
I want the trees to send a breeze
I want to live in those moments
and beg for time to freeze
I want to love my body
and know you love it in return
I want lust to fall for love
and together they can burn
I want someone to understand
that I'm vulnerable but sure
that I want someone to stay
when I say I'm insecure

because I deserve more
than mediocre love, it's true
and the man who I will meet
will deserve more than that too

is it too early to start
thinking of what loving you
will be like?

I let myself love you
as if I haven't been loved before

I let us have the gift of firsts
with the lens of the second

I let us make our mistakes
without the looming of his
anticipating your actions

I let us create a masterpiece
that is entirely our own

I let go
to finally let you in

when you hug me
chest presses to chest
and our hearts cling to each other
beneath the blanket of skin

when you hug me
I forget everything

but the way in which you smell
as my head nestles in your neck
like a home I've always known
but have just recently met

and I look up at your eyes
getting lost in their ocean hue
there is starlight in its daylight
it is a colour more than blue

we are just friends

sometimes we steal glances
and weigh up our chances
of the other ever falling

but we are just friends

intoxicated kisses are just kisses
it does not mean we miss
each other when we go home

we are just friends

I remember everything you say
and I'll go out of my way
to make you smile

because we are just friends

the reason I can see your halls
from my window
doesn't mean anything at all
it is simply a coincidence

because we are just friends

friends who hold each other
when the night gets low

friends who prove they stay
when everyone turns to go

friends who have fallen silently
that they love too deeply

friends who admit they are more
and suddenly feel completely
and utterly in love

maybe we aren't just friends
maybe that has never been enough

to hold the innocence of firsts
with the maturity of experience
and still be ready to love you
makes me realise how special this is

I asked him to kiss me
like a poem he wanted me to write

with soft syllables
and rough edges
that underlined a tone
of everlasting kindness

he loves me gently

with soft circles
that trace galaxies
into my lower back
promising me a universe
in the way he holds me

he loves me enough
that he writes this poetry for me

to anyone else it seems like
I have loved you too quickly

but there are years of memories
disguised with platonic potential
that shape the way I yearn for you

I have learnt how to hide
the way my stomach smiles
with its billions of butterflies

but I don't have to anymore

this time I will love you openly
with lingering kisses
and soft touches of the skin

making up for the time lost
pretending friends was all
we could ever truly be

we were never just friends

perhaps consciously
our morals restricted the thoughts
of us being something more

but our hearts were beating loudly
pleading for us to make our way back home

*we are now home*

how did we not notice
the signs or the string
the way fate laughed
when we ignored everything

miles split us into memory
until we lived outside a door
convincing ourselves its platonic
that it can't be anything more

but my dear we were wrong
losing to the tangle of our fears
for we had both been secretly in love
with each other for all those years

lay down your armour
allow your weapons to drop
let your walls fall
and simply exist with me

I don't know if you've ever
experienced slowly falling in love
with someone the more you speak to them

but it kind of feels like starlight and sunsets
mixed into this body that breathes electricity
it feels magical but also natural
like this is how life is supposed to be
like all the thunder in your head doesn't even know how
to rain anymore and for the first time there is sun

there is someone whose actions and words
make you feel seen and heard
in a way you've never felt before
and suddenly you understand
the poets and the dreamers
you were never a believer
before but now you're devoted

praying to every sign because
you've never known love like this

your touch is magnetic
sending a forcefield
around my heart
so that every fibre
of my soft being
is attracted to you

to be loved for you
feels like learning colour

it isn't exactly yellow
or a mellowed indigo
but a shade that promises
we will always be

I wonder if this colour
was made by you and me

whether we loved hard enough
to cause the lights to blind each other
into something smoother

almost as if the blues and reds
merged with the oranges
to hold each other again

they didn't have to
be separate anymore

they could finally exist together

we are two artists in love

your fingers ache from clicking
my palms sting from clapping
and we do it again and again and again

I catch myself humming your melodies
you find yourself re-reading my book
and we do it again and again and again

little lyrics slip off of my tongue
whilst you name the titles of my poems
and we do it again and again and again

weeks are assorted into open mic nights
and suitcases piled with copies of *healing*
and we do it again and again and again

but the best part of loving an artist
is watching the little moments of love
slip into the intricacies of their work

we become cliches
we become each other's muses
we become each other's rhymes
we become each other's motivation

we become
  we become
    we become

two artists in love

our bodies melt with molten ache
softening at each earthquake
that binds us together

I want you to hold me like this forever

## how it feels to fall in love with your best friend

it begins slowly.

when you're together something simply clicks; a light switch turns on and everything is brighter.

you ignore the rainbows that bloom when you're able to shine a little light on their darker days. you ignore the fact that nobody else brings out that side of you. you ignore the fact that nobody knows that side of you except them.

you ignore the warmth that fireworks through your body. you ignore how beautiful it makes you feel. you ignore it because losing them is worse than loving them from a distance. you ignore it because you're scared.

you ignore it
  you ignore it
    you ignore it

until one day there is too much love
to contain inside your aching fingertips
and you let the love tumble out
impulsive, excited and yearning
and you do not resist
and they do not resist
and nothing changes except
the sound of your love
no longer dimmed to a hum
but sung to anyone who will hear

*I fell in love with my best friend*

I'm in love

stupidly, embarrassingly
head over heels

so much so I've
forgotten how to feel
anything else
but the ache
in my face
from smiling
at the way
we've fallen
into place

like an ending
interwoven into a beginning
a song with lyrics
you can't stop singing
and I keep bringing
myself to hold back
because there was a time
I couldn't love you like that

but now there is nothing blocking me
now there is nothing stopping me
from loving you loudly
and loving you proudly

because I can finally call you mine
because I can finally love you openly this time

when you kiss me
it feels as though
I never knew the notion

it's a soft explosion
of fireflies and butterflies
that dance my world into colour

when you love me
you do so like
no other before

I used to think
I was so sure
of love's definition

but all the fondness
I have ever felt is unlike
the position I am in

I am yours
and I am sure
I have always been

you do not hesitate to love me

commitment doesn't seem like chains
but more like dancing in the rain
forever, together

*I love yous* do not seem too fast
but are words to ensure we last
forever, together

buying flowers isn't a chore
but something to ensure
forever, together

communication isn't unrealistic
but rather you see it as intrinsic
forever, together

and I truly hope we find our
forever, together

the most mundane moments
become magical with you

you are the physical embodiment of music

there are chords in your eyes
that turn the colour blue
into an orchestra of serenity

there are tunings to your smile
sometimes a soft ballad
or a loud explosion of joy
both as beautiful as the other

there are harmonies in your words
not just the register of your tone
but the ability to calm my core
with three simple words

you are the person
I begged the moon for

the person I hoped
I'd dance in the kitchen with
as your hand wraps around my waist
and the sweet smell of cinnamon
lingers in between our kisses

you are the person
I used all my wishes on
every penny in my pocket
delicately thrown in the fountain
waiting for you to arrive

and then you did

now you are the person
I thank the moon for

loving you is like being a child
trying to sleep before their birthday

your lungs swap oxygen for giddiness
and the butterflies dance around your body
smiling at the thought of every possibility

you shut your eyes tight
letting the world rest for a moment
but your mind cannot stop beaming
at what comes next

I think the universe
took a little more care with making you

how your smile curves
itself down before it beams
like a star blinking before its light

how you interlace your fingers
to comb back your hair
like a songbird ready to sing

how your eyes become an entity
when the sun shines on them
like a wave learning how to soothe

there is something fundamentally
meaningful about the way in which you exist
and surely something that magical
cannot be coincidental

*journal entry #2*

I've never known love like this. I will never want to know another love like this. I don't think there is any other romantic love that could exist for me. you are everything I have ever hoped and wished and manifested. you are everything to me. I am so grateful to be loved by you and am so lucky to be in this love. I think that's another thing too. the way I love has never truly been appreciated, or if it has it has never been reciprocated out of pure intention to love rather than to balance. that's the thing with you, you don't love out of convenience or because you're obliged to settle almost a love score, you love because it is the thing you know how to do and want to do. I get it because I am the same. I don't write these things just to seem like I want to send you something. don't get me wrong, I am conscious that I want you to wake up to something nice to read but this also feels incredibly natural just to pour my heart into a message and make your morning start off well. it doesn't feel like something I have to do or should do, it is just something that is done. it's a type of love that is so natural it borders a state of unconsciousness, if not for the irony of the conscious aspects of wanting to make you know you're loved and to go out of my way to make your day.

and suddenly
letting someone in
wasn't as scary anymore

I shook off the walls
I so desperately carved
around my heart
and stood defenceless

*is that all you've got?*
I screamed to love

at first I thought it didn't hear me
and simply let my words scatter
in the same place it broke my heart

but something shifted
like a whisper before the storm
rustling all the people that left
and clearing all I couldn't view

love never spoke that day
but it answered by showing me you

my heart studied the concept
of yearning for years
for to be in love with you
was to enjoy how it ached

I let my hands stretch
fingertips colliding with air
knowing it could hold what
was never allowed to be seen

so I hid *I love yous*
within birthday cards
that poured my heart
into a platonic prison

I just never knew you
were trapped there too

you see me
for everything
I have ever
tried to be

I cannot stop falling
into the safety hues
of the blues
in your eyes

they are more than oceans
and simple soothing skies

but galaxies of hope
wrapped in a soft embrace
it is the type of blue
that even time and space
cannot contain
the type of blue
that quietens my brain
into a lulling melody
it is the type of blue
that becomes my only remedy

it is the type of blue
that cannot be reduced
to the words of a poet

it is the type of blue
that could move mountains
and I think you secretly know it

he simply understands me
without uttering a word

all the worries in my heart
are unspoken yet heard

he does not flinch or flee
but stays close each night

and suddenly he appears
in everything that I write

I'd be happy to only see the world
in the reflections of your eyes

to view the world in fractions
if it meant a lifetime of
being loved in whole

I'd gaze in glimpses
if it meant the view
was kissed by the blues
that make my soul smile

I'd do anything to see the world
in the way in which you do
because maybe it'll show me
why I am deserving of love

there are two toothbrushes by the sink
one for me and one for him
the first is blue, the other pink
it is quite a simple thing
but the notion of having two
in a place that used to be one
suggests that everything we do
is a picture of all that we've done
I will love you for all of the lifetimes
until the final star begins to shrink
I will give you all of my lifelines
through our toothbrushes by the sink

I escape time with you

days lose their concept
the clock in my mind quietens
and all I can hear is you

I do not worry about death
I do not calm my breath
because you are here

we are here

and for this moment
that's all that matters

a kiss is simply a kiss

two lips touching
then pulling away
then touching again

but it was *us* that made it beautiful

that transformed pointless pouting
into constellations and celebrations
of millions of moments that are
held between this bright ache
of our bodies melting into one
and these kisses burning into love
and suddenly feeling enough just from

two lips touching
then pulling away
then touching again

it feels like the firework
that made us
exploded into two halves

*twin flames*
I think they call them

two bodies melting into each other
forming one single essence
that creates something bigger
than the both of them

I pray to experience this life with you

to sink into our wrinkles
and bathe in our ageing skin

I hope that when I complete this life
your hand will be held in mine
and the time comes when
we are old enough to seek it

I pray that we soak up oceans
and dance in the sunsets
that we will watch together

and that we create music
and poetry and scrapbooks
full of the decades spent
loving this life together

if I cannot have forever with you
then I will make this life feel infinite

I will make you feel alive and loved
on the days I am lucky enough
to share this life with you

growing - a definition of poetry

this chapter is like a sunrise.

it is about the dawn of a new day, a new week, a new era. it is about reaching the top of the mountain after so long spent climbing; it is about taking in the view.

whether you've crossed the finish line or are simply questioning if you should begin, allow these poems to invite you to bask in life's sunlight. to hold hope in your palms and believe that there will be a time where things will be better.

what is meant for you will always find you.

if people or moments pass you by then allow them to go. if you were meant to love them, to laugh with them, to get the job, to go on the holiday then you will. until then, trust that everything is working out for you the way that it should.

I've truly found truth in this belief throughout the past year. the people and the moments that did not stay proved to not be worth my energy and everything that did showed me love and light through a new lens. I am so grateful to have felt a rainbow of emotions this year; I wouldn't have been half of who I am now without them.

but that's all part of *growing in*, that everything will be alright.

# Growing In

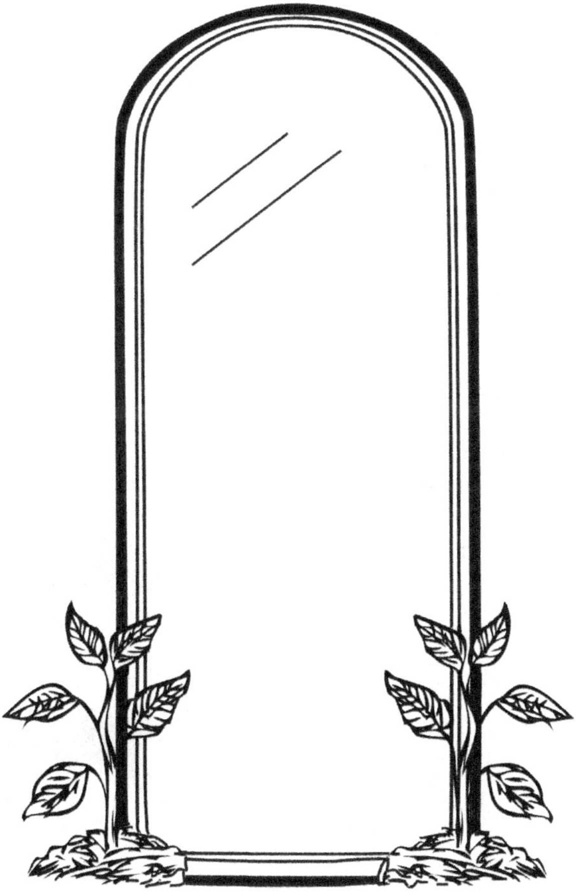

I am so unbelievably tired
of hating the body I was born into

to walk past every shard of glass
and tuck myself back in
like a broken piece
in a forgotten puzzle
trying to find its place

I refuse to do it anymore

this is the year I fall
intentionally in love with myself

this is the year where I love myself
enough to not need
someone to do it for me

this is the year I stop
asking permission to exist

this is the year I become alive

love doesn't have to last forever
for it to have lasted

sometimes it can
just be what it was
and end when it did

that's okay too.

*in some ways*
*I think we were*
*destined to break*

and as I write these words
laughter spills into my ink
as I think about where I stood
only a year before

where I loved you enough
to believe that we were sure
and you loved me enough
to believe that we deserved more

glamorising your pain
won't make it any less real

sobbing on cold tiles at 3am
is not beautiful
it is heart wrenchingly destructive

it cuts poetry into blank verse
it pushes art into irrelevance
it is not pretty

*and it is not supposed to be*

there is nothing idealistic
about the pain they made you endure
there is nothing bright
in the darkness where they deserted you

my dear, stop romanticising
the people that hurt you

you're allowed to look stupid

laugh a little bit too loudly
so that the creases by your eyes
tense up to reflect your smile

dance like everyone's watching
with loose limbs and wide grins
and sing those lyrics proudly

please just lose yourself in the moment

because how people see you
means nothing compared
to the way you view yourself

and it's about time you start seeing
the beauty in simply being you

your new life will cost you your old one

you will have to soak
in oceans of your own sadness
before you can bask in healing's sunlight

you may have to trade the sun
for the softness of the moon for a short while

but to grow you must know
that things cannot stay the same

you must let go

you must know that the life you dream of
cannot remain in the same hue
as the one that has made your life feel broken

you must let your old life go
to step into the warmth of the life
that has been waiting for you

<u>a letter to remind myself who I am…</u>

your heart is crafted like a mosaic; laughter, trauma, memory, poetry - your life is twisted in the emeralds of your eyes. you bleed stardust. you cry galaxies. you exist through your emotions.

do not deny the way you love because you fear you will lose.

remember that a fraction of your existence will be perfection; these moments will be dull in comparison to the colour of life's flaws for you will find beauty in what the world has deemed ugly. you will learn it was never ugly to begin with - it was merely different.

they won't tell you how powerful perception truly is.

your softness sets the pinks of your cheeks alight; a star proud that it still glows despite existing in a deep space.

you do not need to know everything to be okay.

the universe will always be there waiting for you to allow your suns and moons to exist simultaneously.

it is okay if this takes time.

my existence is against all odds
and yet I am here

soaking up sunsets like poetry
and holding on to love like it's a lifeline

and in a way it is

as autumn slips into winter
and loneliness remembers my touch
I embrace the bite of the cold
with the fading memory of joy

*love is keeping me alive*

sometimes the best thing to do is unfollow
untangle the sorrow and stop
getting caught up in knots
of what could have been
and what is no longer true
stop scrolling through their life
that no longer includes you

I bled tears for this kindness
so do not mistake it for weakness

tear stained pillows
and shaking breaths
do not take you back
to their beginning

you have come so far

miles stretch between
your broken heart then
and the fractured heart
that beats for you now

a familiar sadness
does not untangle
all you have learnt

you overcame it then
and *you will again*

do not let loneliness take you back

there is something soft
about your solitude
something reliable

you can fall back on yourself
without having to ask

hold on to that stability

you are living
you are breathing
and *you are here*

loneliness cannot harm you
when you recognise just how
comforting your own company can be

I hold my future
turning in over in my palms
knowing that it'll come
when it is ready

there will always be paths
opening their hearts to you
but it does not mean
you should take them

their ground may have seeped
into the soles of your feet
but it does not mean
you should tread them again

the path may lead to a maze
that guides you to a labyrinth
and you end up where you started
but with less than when you began

and nothing changes
after everything is lost

do not spend the cost
of paths that will not take you anywhere
that you haven't been before

I’ve stopped getting my nails done

the acrylic seeped time
into the beds of my fingernails
and they became weaker
with each attempt to conceal them

so I chose to let them grow

and at first there was no process
nothing more than skin and nail
but suddenly time caught up
and they’ve grown long enough
to be painted blue

maybe everything will be okay too

I used to hate the way
the earth continued to spin
when my world seemed
impossible to live in

but with a shift of focus
I began to notice

that the flowers kept blooming
and the sun kept on smiling
and despite my aching heart
my eyes were finally realising

that each day
is a new way
for me to begin again

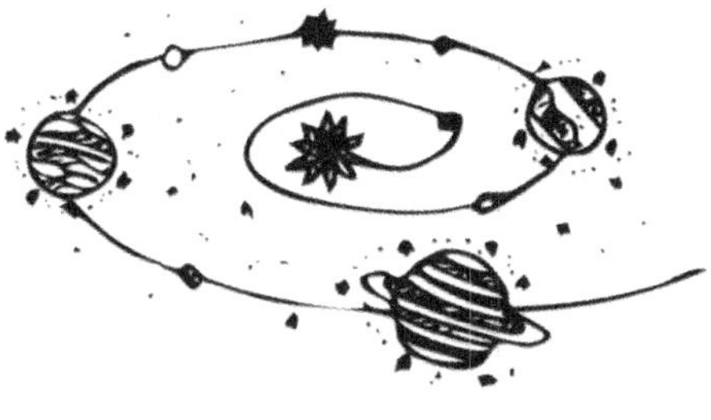

before you love another
you must fall in love
with yourself completely

every scar must take up space
in the home of your affection
you must smile as you catch yourself
in the beauty of your reflection

because you are *perfection*

and this fact has always been true
so fall in love with yourself
before another can fall in love with you

within two weeks
I lost every relationship
I ever knew

and when I looked for 'you'
I realised nobody fit that description
and the only person who would listen

*was me*

and I started to see
that I am not on my own
because as long as I am here
I can never be alone

I have missed the warmth of my heart
that I kept hidden after he left

I thought it was easier to be
colder, tougher
anything other than soft
but in truth it just left me lost

wishing to be found
in the gentle embrace
of my kindness

*oh, it feels good to be back*

I thought numbers mattered

a social group bursting with chatter
all about simple matters
concerning the weather
and whether we liked each other

I thought these were my people

people who plotted my downfall
people who pushed me aside
like I was supposed to be moved

and I accepted it

I fell into the web of whispers
and wielded my own knife
to stab firmly in the spine
before they stabbed it in mine

I became a part of this

woven into the tapestry
each thread sewn like a secret
and I didn't want to keep it anymore

so I took back the energy
I so carelessly loaned to others
and became investing it
into the people that truly matter

first loves
and best friends
all the forevers
they will end

*and that is okay*

we are not supposed
to stay still
we live in a universe
that orbits to will
us into existence

we are moving
evolving
growing
*constantly*

so allow things to end

it is part of who
we are meant to be

it is okay to love as much as you do

do not feel guilty for caring
or loving with an open heart

it is a part of who you are

so please love and lose
and do it all over again
without ever holding back

because you are deserving
of the care that you give others

you are deserving
of your own love

in four years' time
I want to hold sunrises
in the softness of my palms
and be okay with knowing
that the sun will set later

in four years' time
I want to be surrounded by joy
in the form of safe eyes
and a kind smile that laughs
at the little things we do

in four years' time
I want to be grateful for
the seasons that come and go
because I know there a time
I didn't think I'd see them again

you're never too old to enjoy a sunset

because if it doesn't remind you of
of the night you fell in love
then it'll remind you of the night
your mother carried you from the car
into the warmth of your small bed

and if it doesn't remind you
of deliriously laughing
over sleepovers and smores
then it'll remind you of
your grandfather's smile
and the way it lit up a room
with the same crimson hues
that welcome the evening in

and if it doesn't remind you
of the colours a good book
ignites within your heart
then it'll remind you
that despite everything
you are still here
soaking up sunsets like poetry

love exists because you do

you are not the house that broke you
or the friend that forgot you
or the lover that hurt you
or the situation that changed you

their lack of love does not limit
the abundance of yours

you are kindness wrapped
in the hues of your eyes
and the beat of your heart

you are everything you have
always hoped that they would be

how it feels to find yourself again

I am soaking up starlight

dancing in the moonlight
as nebulas bounce off of my eyes

*I am finally alive again*

let the sun finally return
tell him I no longer burn
but instead I now glow

let him know I'm alive

*I'm alive, I'm alive, I'm alive*

nothing lasts

*spoiler alert*
if you didn't know the ending

can't keep pretending
that there is a forever to things
eventually winter turns to spring
and then summer, autumn and back again

things don't stay the same

even though we wish they would
they shouldn't even if they could
because then we would lose our meaning
love has to be lost for love to be worth keeping

can't keep sleeping on the truth
we age from youth
and we tire from love
we pass on and we fade
so there's an ending to us

but that does not mean we should not try
do not be pessimistic and fall into the lie
of 'nothing matters so why do I give it a go'
I said nothing lasts, but the moments mean so
much more than their expiration

this is not an invitation
for you to give up on your dreams
it may seem morbid
but the more it sinks it
you start to realise there is beauty in the fleeting

that our endings give our beginnings
that much more meaning

so *news flash*
present will turn to past

but *spoiler alert*
it's okay that nothing lasts

here's to moving on

raise a glass, lower the flask
and lift your drinks high
toast to the moon and the stars
for everything you've left behind
cheer for who you were and
applaud for who you will become
smile at nostalgia in the corner
and allow her to finally be done
with the shadows and the silence
and the mourning of the past
toast to the people who stayed
and the love that proved to last

you don't have to get over it

you can pull up a chair
and allow grief to sit
if it feels safe in that moment

just don't get too comfortable

allow sorrow to slip in
and the feel anger writhe in your chest
but do your best to remember
that it is temporary

you may wallow until dawn
but the next morning
you must acknowledge the sun

you do not have to get over
the ways they hurt you
just remind yourself that it is done

do not let them pessimists
break your romantic heart

no, write the love letter
even better, write the song
right the wrong and do it again

hold your heart, cradle it like a child
let it run wild and let it fly free

stay up till 3am feeling giddy
let the butterflies roam
let them build homes
around people not places
learn to love their faces
and learn to take up spaces
instead of staying back

learn to love them exactly like that

without guilt, be proud of what you built
all these bricks and rubble
all the light and struggle
cannot break you

do not let them take from you
the way in which you love

and if they cannot handle your love
them leave them out to dry
because someone will come along
and it won't feel like you have to try

we lose 100% of the shots we do not take

so when it comes to love
why do we hold our tongues
mumbling lost syllables
and silencing our passions
in an attempt to 'play it cool'

why do we change the way we love
to be seen as enough
when we lose the best parts of ourselves

why do we not see
that when we limit our heart
we are losing 100% of the starts
to a romance the poets write about

they say I care *too much*

but I think it is rather beautiful
to look at a sunset and see someone
who is no longer on this earth anymore
to love someone with such intensity
that it makes them feel whole again
to hold every emotion in my heart
until it burns because then in turn
I experience life in all its colours
to be able to hear a chord and feel
the music in every bone of my being
to write memory into written magic
and heal myself into growth

I think the way I care
is truly rather beautiful

the drive home was quiet
and my mind thought of you
but the sky held the clouds open
to let the light pass through
and I saw the way its rays
fell upon this quiet evening
and when I looked around
I saw that my life has meaning

*I think I am going to be okay*

to the girl who got broken up with a year ago,

you are still here

though you feared this outcome
it turns out him leaving
was for the best
life gave you a test
and you passed with
success and softness

you were never alone
but were company of your own
and home would soon be found
in other spaces and other faces
and other traces of love
that were not connected to him

you're also no longer angry or hurt
you realise what you deserve
and you hope he is also doing okay
you no longer wish he stayed
but look back fondly on what was
and what shouldn't be again

you held the pain and mourned
and were suddenly reborn
into a new chapter of your life

you started healing
you started feeling
and you were no concealing who you were

life has been a blur
you've found friends
and people in between

you learned what the term
*situationship* means
and my goodness
is it far more complicated
than a six year dated relationship

but you'll get there

people will come and go
sometimes they'll say why
and sometimes you won't know
but you'll learn not to live tied to their string

you will be able to bring
yourself closure
one step closer
than you did before

you'll learn that
there is so much more to this life
when you learn to love your skin
you will learn that he
was not the be all
and end all of everything

and you will move on

life will pass along
and you'll end up in a new city
feeling pretty good
about how the universe works

and it's worth mentioning
that someone ends up
re-entering your day
in a different way
than you allowed yourself to see

you will realise fate
has always meant for you to be
and you will believe that the universe
has rehearsed this life for you

you will love harder than you knew how to

and though a year
may not feel very far
you'll realise you are
so much better where you are

you will look up to the stars
and wish upon the planets
you will be thankful to the way
the universe has planned
your life to go
and you'll know
that even though
life has its endings

the broken paths will mend
and you'll find the road bend
into a new destination
that is the product of all your manifestation

and suddenly the situation
you thought would break you
makes you into someone you always hoped to be

to begin, *thank you.*

the support of both *healing* and *growing* has been beyond what I could have ever expected and I am truly grateful to every single person who has picked up my books and given them a read.

*growing* is most definitely the sequel to *healing*; it continues from the final chapter, following the exit of adolescence and the subsequent beginning of adulthood. it has been a joy to write and illustrate this book, mainly just to preserve the life lessons I have learnt in the past year of writing it; it's almost like my written scrapbook. more importantly, this book became my lifeline in many ways and I am forever grateful to be able to create another piece of art that is so special.

a big thank you to my family for their unwavering support. Mum, you have always taught me strength and resilience; those traits are ubiquitous throughout this book and throughout my life. I love you, you are a light to this world and please never forget that. Dad, you have always believed in what I can do; from my stories as a child to now, you've never doubted me for a second and I am so grateful. Nan, you are truly my biggest supporter. from your friends to the man who fixed our fridge, you never fail to tell people how proud you are of me and everything I do; I am so grateful for having the coolest Nan. Chan, there are many parts of me I wouldn't have grown into without you there to plant the seed. thank you being a part of who I am and for showing me the courage it takes to show up for yourself every day. I am so proud of you. Sam, I am grateful to finally be old enough to learn about the person you are, especially when I find out you introduce me to everyone as your 'brain-box sister'. Most importantly, to my fur babies Tilly and Poppy, thank you for all the cuddles during the creation of this book. to my late Grandad Alan, thank you for always having faith in what I do; I miss you infinitely.

to the love of my life, Arieh, thank you for the way in which you love. you love me like poetry. you love me with intention. you love me into your music. you love me with all of the elements; the fiery passion, the necessity of air, the cooling of water and the grounding of the earth. you love me like it is the easiest thing to do, and I suppose it is. loving you is the most simplest answer to life that I've ever understood. thank you for making me believe that I deserve it. I promise to dedicate every day to making sure you believe you deserve it too.

thank you to my friends for being the foundations of all that I write. this year has truly been one of change, yet each friend I have found along the way has formed the mosaic of who I am.

thank you to my home friends, Libby and Millie (for all the laughter, Toby Carveries and support you've given me over the last year), Maddy (for always reminding each other exactly who we are), Benny and Burak (for never letting time get in the way of picking up where we left off), Aaron and Nathan (for every round of bowling that always ends up in laughter).

thank you to the friends I was lucky enough to find through the vastness of the internet, G and Wezza (you are the most kindest people I know; I am so fortunate for every call and competitive uno games, but I am more grateful for your everlasting support), Isabel (for seeing me better than I often see myself; you are a gift to this world), Grace (for helping to make the most perfect cover to this book, I am so grateful).

thank you to the friends I found at university, Emily (thank you for the 7 hour dinners, angel numbers and friendship that feels like an exhale after so long of holding your breath. thank you for being the most talented person I know; everyone deserves to read the magic which you write - @canvasofthesky), Gee (for the laughter led lectures, the gym sessions where we talk much more than we exercise and the glorious poetry in which you write - @gee_poetry), Issy (for showing me how beautiful female friendships can be), the Flat 12 Family (for every drunk night, bicker, laughter and messy cooking; first year would have been so different without you all and I wouldn't have changed it for a second), Joshi (for being the only person I know to balance chaos and kindness), Noush and Lara (for the Peak District giggles and the love in which you both immediately showed me), Josie (for being the anchor at the places we work together). whether we speak daily or over the occasional pint, thank you for the impact you've all had on this book.

thank you to the most beautiful online community; whether you've engaged with my posts, my performances or read my books, you are all beautiful souls and I am so fortunate for the love in which you all show me. thank you to the live community on TikTok for being a light in the evenings that could often have been darker. to all the poets within our community, please keep writing; the world deserves to hear you.

and finally, I am thankful to the person I have become during the creation of this book. for every heartbreak, change and trial, I found the strength to believe that it would all turn out okay (spoiler alert, it did!).

this book will be published on my 20th birthday, so happy birthday to me! here's to a life full of love, abundance, health, happiness and joy. here's to my twenties!

I hope you all adore this book as much as I did writing it.

all my love,
Becca x

# I've had a few requests about tattoos…

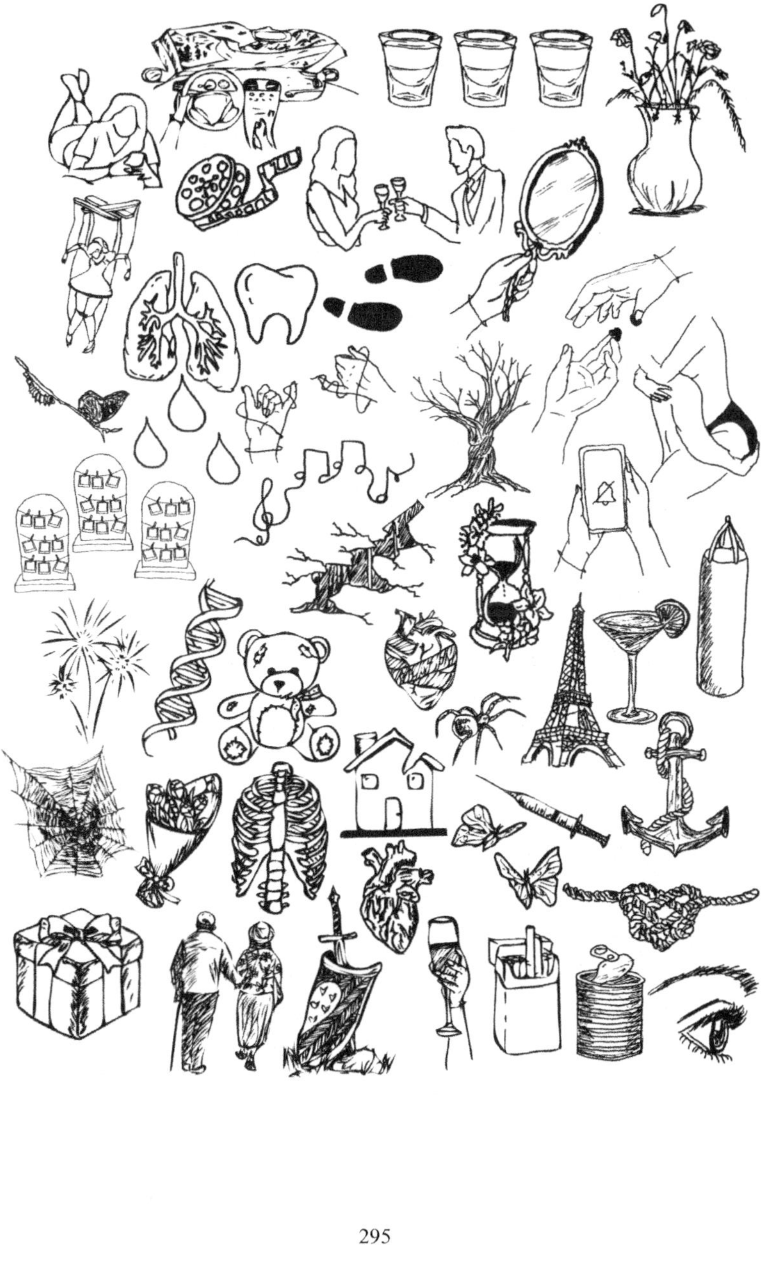

growing - a definition of poetry

Printed in Great Britain
by Amazon

47398897R00169